The Toltec Path of Transformation

The Toltec Path of

Transformation

Embracing the Four Elements
of Change

HeatherAsh Amara

The Toltec Path of Transformation
Embracing the Four Elements of Change

HeatherAsh Amara

Cover design by Kathryn Sky-Peck
Cover art by © Damaratskaya Alena/shutterstock.com

Hierophant Publishing
8301 Broadway, Suite 219
San Antonio, TX 78209
888-800-4240
www.hierophantpublishing.com

If you are unable to order this book from your local
bookseller, you may order directly from the publisher.

Library of Congress Control Number: 2012942550

ISBN 978-0-9818771-9-8
10 9 8 7 6 5 4 3 2 1
Printed on acid-free paper in the United States

*May these words help all beings balance
mind, spirit, emotions, and body
and return to their authentic, divine center.*

Contents

Foreword

by Vicki Noble

The four elements have been recognized and honored for many thousands of years, as can be seen in art and archaeological artifacts from the ancient civilizations of the Americas, Old Europe, Africa, the Middle East, China, India, and Tibet. There are probably as many ways of conceptualizing the four elements as there are different peoples around the world, yet the basic structure remains fundamentally the same. Calling in the water, wind, earth, and fire grounds us in physical reality while opening us in a sacred way.

Regardless of origin, pictorial representations from different cultures share a structure consisting of four sacred or holy beings arranged in the cardinal directions around a central figure or symbol. Some of the earliest Navaho sand paintings on record bear an uncanny resemblance, for example, to ceramic plates that are thousands of years old excavated from sites on the other side of the world in Iran. Similarly, a Navaho sand painting created at a museum in the Southwest in the 1950s depicts "Whirling Rainbow People from Windway" not at all unlike the Tibetan Buddhist concept of "dakinis" (female beings who fly through space) who, when invoked from the four cardinal directions and the center, come whirling in like vases of energy.

In the European tradition, the East represents the element of air and the dawning of consciousness; the Southern lands of the equator suggest fire and noonday passion; the Western ocean points to water and the nostalgic feelings aroused by the sunset; while in the North we see the earth element in the cold regions of the Arctic at midwinter. When Karen Vogel and I made the Motherpeace tarot cards in the late 1970s, we were working with this exact system. Modern shamans "call in" the directions in rituals celebrated on holidays, marking the days of the seasonal calendar that correspond to the same cardinal directions and their intermediary cross-quarter days.

The special gift of this book is the unique synthesis that HeatherAsh is able to make by blending everything she has learned about the elements over the course of her life as a Western spiritual seeker. Speaking directly to her peers, HeatherAsh translates the ancient system into a tool for these faster, more secular times in which we live, offering modern people a way of transforming their lives and releasing the obstacles that block their way to serenity and well-being. She offers advice and encouragement every step of the way, sharing stories from her own experience and observations from her work with students, grounding the teachings in the day-to-day struggles of real people in today's world.

HeatherAsh's approach offers an accessible path in these urgent times. The simplicity of it makes it possible for people to use the method in spite of being overwhelmed by other obligations. Imagine, if each of us could find his or her way back to the center of our own being with the help of the healing power of elements, we might generate peace and love on this planet! May it be so for every reader of this book, and may the principles and practices of the four directions be alive and well in our lives once more.

Blessed Be.

Acknowledgments

My gratitude goes out to the many people who have supported me over the years.

First, to my parents, Jerry and Maggie Gaudet, and to my sister, Christy, who held such a strong container for a childhood of adventure and travel. I love you.

Many blessings to my teachers and guides over the years: Vicki Noble, Cerridwen Fallingstar, Peggy Dylan, Ana Forrest, and don Miguel Ruiz. Don Miguel, I am so grateful for all of your teachings, deep wisdom, and friendship. Deep gratitude to my friend Gini Gentry for your amazing cheerleading and love and helping me find my own path.

To my first circle sisters, Autumn Labbe-Renault, Isis Ward, Saurin Shine, Sana Banks, Heather Wahanik, Aimee Carroll: Yes!

To all friends—past, present, and future—for being teachers and inspirations, especially my favorite family and kids, Autumn, Craig, Rowan, Kyra, and Nash Labbe-Renault; Jesikah Maria Ross, Thom Sterling, the Normal family, and WEF.

Thanks and praise to the original Toltec Center

board and teachers in Berkeley, California, including Ruth Masterson, Jordan King, Eleanor Mahood, Storm Florez, Francis Hayhurst, Kevin Flores, Audrey Lehman, Kim Christensen, Michele Murphy, Rachel Ohliger, and Dakini Kalhoff.

To my first Toltec family for being such beautiful mirrors, especially Larry Andrews, Ted and Peggy Raess, Chuck and Tink Cowgill, Francis Puerto-Hayhurst, Allan Hardman, Jules J. Frank, Ed Fox, Siri Gian Singh Khalsa, Stephen Collector, Rita Rivera, Gary van Warmerdam, Leo van Warmerdam, Barbara Simon, Niki Orrietas, Roberto Paez, Gae Buckley, Sheri Rosenthal, and Stephanie Bureau; Lee McCormick and all the family of The Ranch and Spirit Recovery; and many others: *Que tu sol sea brillante.*

Gratitude to the incredible team at Toci Austin and Global: Diana Adkins, River Menks, Nikko Bivens, Shiila Safer, Amy Zielinski, Mary Eck, Laura Toups, and so many more, past and present. You know who you are, and I am grateful. And to my fellow dreamers and creators at Wisdom University: Will Taegel, Judith Yost, Jim Garrison, Teresa Collins, and Bob Meyer. Thank you for teaching and sparking me in so many beautiful ways as we co-create conscious community.

Blessings to Randy Davila and the Hierophant Publishing staff for bringing this book back into publication for the second time. Randy, you are a wonderful role model, and I feel very blessed to be playing in this dream with you.

To T for your friendship, giggles, and our ongoing

adventures and explorations, both in the kitchen and out in nature. To Stephen Seigel for being such an amazing dream wrangler, friend, and support over all these years. And a high five to Miguel Ruiz Jr. for your upcoming book and many more collaborations.

Overflowing gratitude to Raven Smith for your immense heart, love, and deep support. Dearest one, thank you for sharing your light and inspiring and catalysing me in so many ways.

Introduction

Four New Allies

Every human has four endowments—self
awareness, conscience, independent will,
and creative imagination. These give us
the ultimate human freedom . . . The
power to choose, to respond, to change.

—Stephen Covey

Have you ever had your world turned upside-down in an instant?

Or struggled to re-align with a big change in your life?

Or wished that some aspect of your life would shift?

Being in a physical form means that you are constantly invited to adjust to change, whether joyous or frightening. From your first lost tooth to your first heartbreak, from a child's graduation to the loss of a friend, from starting a new job to adjusting to a chronic illness, life continues to flow and sometimes gently, sometimes abruptly can alter the landscape of your being.

How you adapt to the changes in your life can mean the difference between being in states of struggle and fear or sweet ease and faith. The simple truth is that when you fight change, you suffer. When you embrace change, you open to creativity, possibility, and healing.

Change is inevitable, but transformation is by conscious choice. While you do not always have control over how or when the changes will occur in your life, you *can* choose how you behave in relation to those changes. When you step toward rather than ignore, fight, or resist change, you reclaim your personal freedom. You step onto a path of transformation and move from being a victim *of* change to being a cocreator *with* change.

Sometimes, whether you are cocreating with or feeling victimized by your circumstances, there are times when change is as elusive as dry land during a flood. Can you remember a time when you wished, prayed, intended, begged, or pleaded for a change to happen, and nothing seemed to budge? Perhaps you felt stagnant, impotent, frustrated, or bewildered. Those times when nothing works and the wheels of change seem to be stuck in the mud are valuable opportunities to go deeper into yourself and awaken unused inner resources. *The Toltec Path of Transformation* will give you the tools and the inspiration to skillfully ride the big waves of change and the courage to delve deep to find the spring of hope within you when nothing else seems to work.

This book blends the shamanic elements of traditions from around the world with the transformational teachings of the Toltec, specifically through don Miguel Ruiz, author of *The Four Agreements*. Many beings have walked before us on their own paths of transformation, and when we are willing to slow down and turn to their wisdom, we may find answers to many of the issues that keep us unbalanced and overwhelmed or stuck and stagnant. Our human ancestors never had to deal with keeping up with emails, crashing stock markets, or the sometimes overwhelming complexity of the twenty-first century; they had many gifts derived from their close relationship to nature and the cycles of life that are eternally relevant—and I believe vital—to us modern humans.

We'll start at the beginning, with the elemental building blocks of life. Then we will explore the sacred teachings embedded in the seasons and learn how the elements are also reflections of the four most important aspects of our being.

The Elemental Foundation of Life

The elements of air, fire, water, and earth are the cornerstones of life. From the air you breathe to the earth beneath your feet, from the water you drink to the heat of the sun, each of the elements is vital to your very existence. Without just one of these elements, all life on the planet would cease to exist.

Native peoples around the world have always honored the four elements as ever-present allies. From Native American traditions to the roots of Buddhism, from African ritual to European shamanic wisdom, the elements of air, fire, water, and earth are at the core of every spiritual tradition. By opening to the wisdom passed down through the lineages of native peoples, you will learn how to use the elements as a framework for a new way of being in relationship to change.

The four elements are powerful guides for how to live in alignment with nature and your own essence. Every breath of air can bring more spaciousness into your being. Fire invites you to expand into more vibrancy and brilliance. You can learn how to become fluid like water. The earth against your feet reminds you to be fully in your body. Each element is a tool for becoming more present and vital.

When you consciously align with the four elements, you will release what no longer serves you and tap into the wisdom of life itself.

In the next chapter, you will learn how to make the four elements powerful allies of transformation in your life. But first, let's continue exploring the building blocks of conscious change.

Living within the Cycles

Change is not linear but a never-ending spiral process of inspiration, fruition, deepening, death, and rebirth. The four main markers of the year—spring equinox (air), summer solstice (fire), fall equinox (water), and winter solstice (earth)—reflect how change actually occurs in nature and in humans.

In ancient times, individuals and communities shared in the cyclical changes of nature by gathering to celebrate the equinoxes and solstices. Every part of the cycle, from recent deaths to the new births, was honored. Coming together in community gave all individuals a pause from their day-to-day life to witness the cycles of change in their community and a marker to notice what had changed for them internally since the last gathering. This allowed them to feel part of a whole and to choose where they wanted to put their energy in the coming months.

In modern times, you might feel a sense of separation from the cyclical nature of change. Electric lights, fixed work hours, and linear thinking all distance you from the ebb and flow of the natural world. With the more recent ability to communicate instantaneously with one another via email and cell phones, you might believe that internal transformation or external change should happen this instant. The result of this kind of mental pressure is frustration, self-judgment, and confusion. When you align with the seasons of nature and the four elements, the result is flow, faith, and patience.

Let's explore the wisdom of the elemental cycles of nature with a little journey through the seasons. Each season has a gift to share that you can apply to embracing and fostering ease-filled, effortless change.

The Four Seasons of Change

Whether or not you live in an area that has four distinct seasons, these four quarters of the year are tangible metaphors for the cycles of change that touch us all. As you read through each description, use your imagination and senses to feel the quality of each season. Open to each element associated with the seasons and reflect on the importance of each turn of the cycle in your life experiences.

Spring

Imagine a beautiful spring day, when tiny green buds start exploding on tree branches like popcorn, and multi-colored tiny flowers wave and dance in lush grasses. The breeze feels like silk pajamas, and the sky shimmers with the increasing warmth.

Spring is the time of new beginnings and is associated with the element of air. In spring, seedlings poke their delicate heads through the darkness of soil and into the air of the boundless sky. Babies are born and take their first precious breaths. New life sprouts joyfully, wide-eyed and curious.

All change begins with a seed of thought or focus. Everything humans have created, from tires to stories, first begins as a thought or a flash of inspiration. Your thoughts are immensely powerful, and seeds of thought can germinate and grow rapidly, even the ones that don't serve you. Spring teaches you to have clear vision to perceive which thoughts arise from your fears and which arise from your truth.

Summer

Imagine yourself on a summer's day, drinking the sunlight into every pore and tasting the bright yellow-orange fullness of a just-picked peach. The days are long, and the sun is at its fiery fullest, blessing everything with its heat and light. Summer brings vibrant growth and tremendous energy. This is a time of rapid expansion and juicy ripening as the flower turns to fruit and ripens into its full sweetness.

Summer is associated with the element of fire. The heat of the sun warms up life's passion, creativity, and enthusiasm, and we see this vibrancy reflected in the red rose and the bountiful fruit heavy on the trees.

If you want to keep your spring seedling of change

alive, you need to give it light and heat in the form of your energy, or action. Without proper attention, your baby inspirations will not get what they need to grow, or they will be crowded out by weeds and distractions. This is the season for action. One vital need now is for good weeding to give your seedlings a chance to mature and prosper.

In your own process of transformation, this part of the cycle is for gathering and consolidating your energy and clearing away anything that saps your vitality and focus.

Fall

As the light of summer fades into fall, we welcome the rains and the turn toward darkness. Imagine yourself in a forest surrounded by red and golden leaves fluttering down from the trees, a light mist on your face, and the autumn sun starting to set with a sigh. You can feel the fast pace of summer seeping out of your bones, and you begin to turn inward, your blood slowing down like the sap in the trees.

Fall is associated with the element of water. Leaves fall from the trees like rain, and storms come, filling the creeks and rivers and decorating the trees and plants with crystalline drops of liquid. In the ebb and flow of life, fall shifts us toward the ebb of our seasonal cycle.

Fall is a time of reflection and harvest. Once we have clarified our vision and cleaned away any obstacles, we move into a time of deepening. We have the opportunity to reflect on our initial intent and either energize it or release it. Fall reminds us to soften and be with the changes that are happening. Just as the trees do not clutch onto their leaves in fear of being exposed, we learn to open our hands and surrender to change.

This is a time for harvesting the ripe fruit of our intent, which sometimes does not look as we had expected. As we release our expectations and become present with the aroma and shape of our creation, we can taste its perfection.

Winter

Now imagine that winter has come, and the trees surrounding you are bare, like skeletons anchored in the earth. Snow muffles your footsteps and empties the land around you of animals, color, and sound. The cold causes you to pull inside to your core, and you can feel the wisdom of the hibernating bears and trees as they draw into themselves, seeking nourishment from their depths. The land is stark and silent, but in the silence, you feel your soul being fed.

Winter is a time of rest, of death and rebirth. The element associated with winter is earth. The trees are stripped down to their essential bones, and the snow-covered mountains or the bare earth dominates the landscape.

During winter, the earth goes dormant, and we move into the longest night of the year. In the cycles of life, rest and death are a vital part of change. When you are manifesting intent, you always need time to rest and reflect. This period of rest helps you to see what must be let go to move on. Perhaps you need to accept the death of outdated beliefs, relationships, or ways of perceiving yourself. This is a time for nourishing yourself in silence and reflecting on the changes and growth you have made. Winter teaches you to pull inward so that you can offer your gifts from the most essential nature of who you are.

As you reflect, you can choose to release your initial intent and plant the seed of a new purpose or reenergize your original intent, making it stronger and more focused for the next cycle. In this time of silence, it may appear that nothing is happening. But deep within the earth a new seed has been planted. It is gathering and storing energy, nourishing itself for the coming burst of energy to sprout in the spring.

Deep Change, Deep Honoring

Each season is heralded by a day that marks the transition between one quarter and another: the equinoxes and solstices. At the vernal and autumnal equinoxes (March 20, 21, or 22 and September 20, 21, or 22), the earth and sun are in perfect balance; day and night are the exact same length, and the sun shines directly on the equator. In the Northern hemisphere, summer solstice (June 21) is the longest day of the year and the start of the summer season; winter solstice (December 21) is the longest night of the year and the start of the winter season. For the Southern hemisphere, this is just the opposite; winter solstice is on June 21, and summer solstice is December 21.

Here is a great lesson from the seasonal transitions. While a definite shift in the relationship of the sun to the earth and day and night occur at each of the quarter days of the solstices and the equinoxes, these concrete changes are not noticeable immediately. The day after the winter solstice—the longest night of the year—there is more light than the day before. But you do not wake up on December 22 (or June 22 in the southern hemisphere) and say, "Hey, look; there is more light today! The sun is returning!" A change has occurred, but the change has not become manifest yet.

Change follows this pattern in your life as well. You might make a big shift in your life internally, but you may not see the manifestation of this change for months or even years. Change happens below the surface, before there is any visible progress.

These cycles of activity and rest, new growth and harvest, mirror the process of manifesting any desire. There is a season to rest and nourish, and there is a season for action. As you honor all parts of the cycle of change, from birth to death, you will find a deep sense of peace and a new sense of balance.

Balanced Living

Now that you have a new framework for the elemental building blocks of life and the cycles of the seasons, we can add in another layer of insight for how to consciously cultivate change: the four aspects of self.

When you struggle to consciously manifest what you desire (whether this is enlightenment or doing better in school or getting stabilized again after a divorce), it is most likely due to your being out of balance internally. Just as the four elements sustain life, and the four seasons compliment and balance each other, within you are four parts of self that function best when brought together as a whole.

You can bring yourself back to balance by using the four elements as reflections of the different aspects of yourself. Just as one of the elements is not more or less important than any other, no one part of you is more or less important.

The four aspects of self are your mental body (air), your energetic body (fire), your emotional body (water), and your physical body (earth).

Like many of us, you probably have a tendency to rely on one part of yourself and dismiss the others. For example, in the Western world, we place great emphasis on the power of the mind and minimize the wisdom of the emotions and intuition. Many of today's main religions create a split between the physical body and the spiritual being. Any kind of schism between the four parts of self creates conflict within.

For the Toltecs in Teotihuacan, Mexico, which is called "the place where humans become divine," the elements were used as guideposts of transformation. The huge pyramid complex of Teotihuacan was designed as a physical reflection of the inner journey to connect with divinity and authenticity.

People follow the path of initiation from the plaza of earth, where they symbolically bury their physical bodies, then move through the plaza of water to release the emotional body, the plaza of air to free the mental body, and the plaza of fire to ignite the spiritual body. This process purifies and aligns the self-direct experience of being in the flow of universal energy, or life.

Following the wisdom of the Toltecs and many other native peoples, you can use the four elements as cornerstones to rebuild your "house," based on the foundation of your authentic self. As you integrate your mind, energy, emotions, and body into full awareness, you will set into motion deep internal healing and growth.

In the next chapter, we will go into detail about the importance of remodeling your inner house to foster change and connection, from the smallest adjustments to the biggest transformations.

1

Remodeling Your Inner House

In oneself lies the whole world and if
you know how to look and learn, the
door is there and the key is in your hand.
Nobody on earth can give you either the
key or the door to open, except yourself.

—Krishnamurti

Imagine yourself as a house; your mind, spirit, emotions, and body are the four corners of your foundation. Is your base stable and supportive? Do your closets have clutter? Are the rooms in your house decorated exactly they way you want? Is there space and light and peace throughout?

Or is your internal house in need of a good cleaning and some major remodeling?

Actually, you have been building the house of yourself since childhood, often based on other people's designs. If you had all the resources necessary to remodel your life, how would you choose differently? What walls would you tear down? How would you want your house to feel?

The Toltec Path of Transformation shares the steps to an internal remodeling that will improve all aspects of your life—from your work to your home to your health, from your inner relationship with yourself to your outer relationships with friends, partners, and family. No matter how severe or minor the changes you want to make in your life, this book will support you in making positive, concrete shifts in the actual structure of your being. Remodeling takes tools and skill, and *The Toltec Path of Transformation* will guide you step by step in gaining the awareness, energy, and courage to build the life you have always wanted to live.

Remodeling begins by delving into the old structure. Parts of your current house, or self, were created unconsciously and now no longer serve you. But which walls need to come down, and what will anchor you during the renovation?

Although remodeling oneself can be exhilarating, it is also disruptive. This book offers the perspective and tools of a seasoned home-transformation guide to make your remodeling as easy as possible. As you rearrange and take down old structures, you will learn how to call on the four elements to be your scaffolding, or support, and a safe container for change. The elements will empower you to rebuild your life on a strong, balanced foundation.

Change, no matter how eagerly awaited, is unsettling and involves a loss, a sacrifice of something. Moving is the loss of an old way of living. Aging is the loss of youth. From being laid off your job to getting sick to coming home from a great vacation, all transformation creates instability and takes a period of readjustment.

What inner or outer transitions are you in right now? What are you remodeling within and without?

By learning the tools and the skills necessary to remodel yourself, you can consciously tear down the walls of limiting beliefs and clear inner blockages to create more space and beauty in all the transitions of your life. You will learn to reclaim lost or stagnant energy, step fully into your power, and feel supported and vitalized by life. Your inner house will transform from a cluttered, cramped single-wide to a light-filled, spacious reflection of your heart and soul.

Are you ready?

Whenever you begin any remodeling project, the first step is to assess the stability of the current structure. Most likely, the floors of your internal house do not solidly rest on an abiding connection to your authentic self but are precariously balanced on false beliefs, or agreements, that you created or were told as a child. It is this shaky internal foundation that causes anxiety, fear, and a feeling of scarcity.

Hand in hand with assessing the current structure of being is opening to your vision of what is possible. What is the end result you are looking for from your internal remodeling project? More love? More peace? More laughter? More stillness? You get to choose the colors, patterns, and lighting in the sacred creation of your inner home.

Let's start by looking at how these structures are created early in our life, sometimes from tiny events that have a huge impact on our thoughts, feelings, and actions. Once we understand the mechanics of how our old house was built, we have the knowledge to then roll up our sleeves and rebuild ourselves from the inside.

The Structures That Bind Us

Pretend that you are three years old, and you are playing rambunctiously with your eight-year-old brother. Feel your excitement as you laugh and gleefully run around the house, arms waving, feet barely touching the ground.

Suddenly, you hear a loud noise behind you, and you turn to see that your brother has accidentally knocked over a vase, which has shattered all over the floor.

How would you react?

Imagine that you both freeze and look at each other,

wondering what to do next. Your brother shakes his head and says, "We'd better clean this up before mom gets home," but when you go into the kitchen to get the broom, you both decide to have a snack first. Before long, the two of you are laughing and playing again, forgetting all about the vase.

Your mom is on her way home and has had a rotten day. She had an argument with her boss, she's been stuck in traffic, she is running late, and the chocolate bar she's been thinking about all has day melted on the seat of her car. Mom is definitely *not* having a good day.

Then she checks her voicemail and hears a message from her new babysitter, who says, "I'm sorry; I tried to call you earlier. I have to leave a bit early today because Wednesdays are the day I go to cheerleading practice, but the kids should be fine . . ."

Mom's not-good day just got worse.

So you can imagine Mom's state when she walks through the door and hears you and your brother laughing and running around; then sees her grandmother's vase—the only thing her grandmother had ever given her—shattered on the floor.

What is her reaction?

Let's pretend that Mom has rarely yelled or gotten upset with her kids, but today she just loses it. She starts yelling, "Who broke my vase?! Who broke my vase?!"

You and your brother come running into the front room to see what Mommy is yelling about. You are both scared when she shouts at you about the vase, demanding to know who broke it.

Your brother looks at you and says, "She did it!"

You look at your brother and then at your mother, stuttering, "I . . . I . . . I didn't—"

"You! Go to your room now!" Mom yells at you.

Close your eyes for a moment and really imagine that you are that child and that you have just been punished for something you didn't do.

How do you feel?

You would probably have a strong emotional reaction, a feeling in your body that fills you from head to toe. You might be angry at your brother for blaming you and upset that your mother would believe him. You may feel scared or confused that your mother has blamed you.

Can you imagine going to your room, sitting on your bed, and saying this to yourself? "Wow, Mom was in a really bad mood! I hope she's okay. And Brother, he must have been really scared when he heard Mom yelling. He must have thought he was going to get in big trouble. Well, I will talk to both of them later and straighten it out."

Would it be possible for you as a small child to have this experience, shrug your shoulders, and sit down to color in your favorite book while waiting for Mom to calm down?

Yes, it is possible, but not likely. . . .

What is more likely (and I'll share why in a moment) is that you have an emotional response like anger, confusion, or sadness. As a young child, you might not even have a word for what you are feeling, just an overwhelming sensation in your body, such as a churning in your stomach, a tightness in your throat, or a tearing feeling in your chest.

The emotion itself is not the problem, but what we do next creates the fodder for most of our ongoing suffering as adults.

We tell ourselves a story.

As a little kid, what would you tell yourself to help you make sense of why your mom sent you to your room for something your brother did?

Over the years of sharing this make-believe scenario with my students, I have made a list of the key points from the stories that they envisioned:

- Mom loves Brother more than she loves me.

- If I lie, I won't get punished.

- It's not safe to play; I'll get in trouble.

- I can't trust Mom.

- I have to be extra careful to be loved and feel safe.

- I'm bad.

- Material objects are more important than people.

- Life's not fair.

Each of these thoughts could be like a dandelion puff blowing in the wind and not taking root, or the puff could land on fertile soil and start growing. These tiny thoughts have immense power—not their own power but the power we give to them.

We are incredible creators, but what we often create is based on the seeds of false thoughts that, when planted, take root and blossom into *agreements*. As don Miguel writes in *The Four Agreements Companion Book:* "Imagine every agreement is like a brick. Humans create an entire structure out of bricks, and we glue it together with our faith. We believe without doubt in all the knowledge inside that structure. Our faith gets trapped inside that structure because we put our faith in each agreement. It's not important if it is or isn't true; we believe it, and for us it is true."

Let's continue to explore how the seed of a thought grows into a story that hardens into a structure that separates you from your center. Once again, imagine yourself as this little kid. Let's pretend that you have the thought, *I got punished because Mom loves Brother more than me.* While it might feel awful to think this thought, can you notice that there is also a sense of relief at having a reason for being punished, even if it is not true?

Imagine that Mom comes into your room and apologizes for yelling at you. She says all the "right" things: "I'm so sorry, honey. I had a rotten day, and I loved that vase, so I got upset. Your Brother just told me that he knocked over the vase by accident and that it wasn't your fault. I love you, and I'm sorry I yelled at you and sent you to your room. Come on, let's go to dinner."

But a little doubt has already been planted in your mind. As you sit down to dinner, imagine that Mom passes the mashed potatoes to Brother first. If you are still holding onto the thought that *Mom loves Brother more,* what would you now say to yourself?

Your oh-so-helpful brain would do what we call selective-evidence gathering. *Aha!* you might say to yourself, *I knew it! Mom passed the mashed potatoes to Brother first. She does love him better.* And later, if Mom passes you the ice cream first, what might you do with that evidence? Often when we have a seed thought and we begin to gather evidence to make sense of the thought, if there is an experience that does not support the story, we actually ignore it, or we weave it into our new story. In this way, we are ingenious! So as a child you might say, *Yeah, Mom passed me the ice cream first, but it is just because she is feeling guilty that she loves Brother more.*

Do you see how you can take one little seed of doubt and build a whole elaborate structure, a fortress, created by ideas and conditions and agreements of what is true and what is not?

Mom likes Brother better, but I don't care anyway. I don't need anyone. Mom likes Brother better because I am bad. Mom likes Brother better because boys are more important than girls. Maybe if I am perfect, if I try really hard, then I'll be loved like my brother is. Or maybe if I am invisible, if no one sees me and I am really quiet and nice, I won't get in trouble.

The situation with the vase is a relatively minor trauma. The child in this scenario might not even remember the incident when she grows up. But you can see what a huge impact it could have on her entire life. The seeds of this new internal structure—*I am bad, I don't need anyone, boys are more important than girls*—will sprout and grow as long as she is not conscious of them. She will literally create a reality that will grow from this handful of unconscious childhood agreements. These beliefs became a shaky floor for all her future actions.

Where have you mistakenly erected jail-like walls based on past stories that limit your current perception and your choices?

The good news is: You do not need to know exactly how you created your structure. All you need to do is tell yourself the truth about the current state of your internal house and remodel yourself from a new foundation.

But there is a secret, an important bridge, between releasing the old and reclaiming the new that few people understand. Here is the insight I discovered that changed everything.

Creating the Life You Want

The hammer and nail tools of this book come from the most potent and practical tools from a variety of spiritual traditions, combined with my own personal experience. I was blessed to study shamanic healing with Vicki Noble, co-creator of the *MotherPeace Tarot*, and to study and teach with don Miguel Ruiz, author of *The Four Agreements*. My apprenticeship with don

Miguel began in 1994, when I approached him to teach me about the tarot. At that time, I did not know that my work with the Toltec community would irrevocably change my life.

From don Miguel, I learned not only the theory but also the practical steps of the Toltec path, which helped me to remodel the shaky floors of my fears and rebuild my inner house from the foundation of my true nature.

But it wasn't easy.

My own healing journey from an unconscious to a conscious structure began more than twenty years ago. Over the course of years of therapy, spiritual work, traveling, and teaching countless workshops, I noticed an interesting pattern in my life. My emotional breakthroughs or "healing—aha!—moments" were often followed by periods of depression, fear, and self-doubt.

Not long after I broke through a fear, it would grab me around the ankles and haul me back to old behaviors. The structure of my old self was still alive and unwilling to change. I wondered if most people had similar experiences and if there was a way to facilitate a lasting change in structure while remaining centered.

As the story above shows, as children we learn to behave in certain ways that often cause us to go against our very nature. It would seem that it would be effortless to release old structures and reclaim our natural, enthusiastic, joyful self.

But even when you consciously choose to change your structure and remodel your inner house, you may experience a great sense of fear and loss. The old agreements obviously no longer serve you. Your actions and behaviors clearly need to change. But when you begin to dismantle or rearrange the old structure, a force seems to stop or divert you.

Sometimes, the closer you get to making a change, the less attractive it seems. You get distracted. You are thrown into chaos and even experience a sense of help-less terror. Or you find yourself getting very sleepy and dull.

So what is the missing ingredient to deep transforma-tion?

In 1999, I dedicated six months to intensely watch-ing this reluctant-to-change part of myself and tracking it in my students. While much had changed for the better in my life, a few deeply rooted issues kept me out of balance. For example, even though I knew better, I clung to a relationship long after I would have been better off ending it. Even though my path was clearly taking me in another direction, I longed to go back to my old spiri-tual community, fearing I might miss out on something. Although my old life was shifting, I resisted the change. I continued to look outside myself for answers, and, to feel safe, I still tried to control other people's behavior.

I kept asking myself: "How do we step out of our limitations? Why do we keep going back to old behav-iors, old relationships, and old ways of reacting? What is the key to lasting personal change?"

When we bring curiosity, patience, and openness to the questions in our lives, answers arrive in a multitude of forms. Mine came in a dream that crystallized years of work with many different teachers, healers, and spiritual traditions. The dream showed me a pathway to living a balanced life in the midst of great inner change. The pathway involved using the four elements to help me reclaim a sacred, possibility-centered life.

The dramatic shifts in my life and in the lives of the many people I've worked with are the direct result of working with these four simple actions based on the four elements, which accelerate and support deep, lasting change.

The Toltec path is about taking responsibility for all of your actions, disrupting routines and habitual ways of perceiving and acting to come back into choice in every moment. This means using whatever tools work the best in your quest for transformation. *The Toltec Path of Transformation* is a synthesis, a flower grown from the soil of much direct experience, guidance, and experimentation. These Four Elements of Change reflect a gathering of the most powerful tools from many spiritual traditions, including Toltec wisdom, European shamanism, and Buddhism. This book integrates the most direct and practical spiritual and healing practices I have found and provides a conscious structure designed to create a container for rapid growth.

In the next chapter, I offer you the vision about regaining authenticity and choice that the elders shared with me in the dreamtime. The insights from this dream form the core of *The Toltec Path of Transformation* and are the heart of the Four Elements of Change.

2

A New Dream, a New Path

We are the living links in a life force that
moves and plays around and through us,
binding the deepest soils with the farthest
stars.

—Alan Chadwick

The Dream of the Elders

I'm standing in a vast, soft-green meadow in a circle of elders, embraced by a wide, violet-blue sky.

"At any moment, you have the capacity to merge fully and completely into your center," one of the elders says.

"This takes a tremendous amount of focus, for it means stepping through your limiting structures," another says, looking directly into my eyes. "As individuals and in community, humans are at the cusp of a great change. The four elements of air, fire, water, and earth will guide people to embody their authentic selves."

A woman steps forward, then leads me to a circle of stones. "Feel the tremendous love and clarity that arises from living out of your true center," she says, inviting me to step inside and sit in the center of the circle. "Honor each element—air, fire, water, and earth—and it will share its wisdom with you."

As I sit on the warm earth, I offer a prayer to welcome the elements to teach me. I suddenly feel a presence in front of me and open my eyes to see a being dressed in soft yellows and gold. As she changes into a golden eagle and soars above my head, I know she is the representation of the element of air. She flies lower and lands on my shoulder, and I discover I can see through her eyes. I feel great peace, and a vastness of vision enlarges all my senses.

"Air represents your mind," she whispers.

I feel a shift within me that allows me to witness clear

mind. Through the bird's eyes, the mind is a place of vision. The mind rests quietly, witnessing all that occurs. As the eagle flaps her wings, the clarity dissolves, and I see my mind out of balance. Everything becomes cluttered and loud. Voices compete for attention. My mind judges everything it sees, including itself. Clear vision is replaced by confusion. I feel fearful and alone.

"The gift of air is clear perception," I hear, and suddenly I can witness my mind without being drowned by its fears. "See with the eyes of the eagle. Align your mind with your center. Let the mind be supported by all of your being."

As the eagle dissolves, I allow her words to touch my core. A few moments later, I feel another being enter the circle. I turn to my right and find myself facing a huge, fiery panther.

"The gift of fire is cleansing," the panther says, arching its back. "Fire represents your spirit, your energetic body." As the panther stretches out a paw and softly brushes my hand, my body lights up with tendrils of energetic fire. I can see the places where my energy burns clearly and the places where an inner structure blocks the flow of energy. My body tingles as energy rushes through and around it.

"Use the fire to clean what does not serve you," the panther says, taking a blocked part of my energy and feeding it to the fire. "Let your spirit shine brightly and align with your center." As the panther becomes a pure flame, I continue to watch my blocked energy burn away.

Another being emerges in the circle to my right. A

man made of water greets me. Inside him, I can see many forms of water: rain, tears, waterfalls, rivers, the ocean, the lightest mist. "Water represents your emotional body," he says, as simultaneously every emotion flows through him. "The gift of water is openness."

Within my body, I feel that everyplace that has ever been closed is suddenly open. I become pure flow, pure emotion. There is no difference between grief and joy. I feel enormous space in my body, and water flows around my structure, creating openings and fissures.

"When you open, great change occurs. Open and find balance." The water man becomes a raging river, a gentle stream, then a clear bowl of pure crystal water. As I drink from the bowl, pure emotion touches my center.

I now turn to face the last element, that of earth. A snake appears and leads me down a hole, deep into the soil. "It is from here that you nourish the seed of your true self," the snake whispers. "I represent earth and the strength of the physical body. The gift of earth is nourishment."

As the snake speaks, I become a tree with roots deep in the earth. I feel in my body what nourishes me and what poisons me; what in my world is food and what is toxic.

"You instinctively know what feeds your center and what feeds your structure. Choose wisely," the snake says.

As I transform from the tree back into my human body, I feel a deep sense of wonder. I can sense all four elements illuminating my own center. They create a new structure that surrounds and holds me. I no longer feel alone or confused.

Once again, I am standing in the circle in the meadow with the elders. They speak to me of the journey of change: "To become the butterfly, a caterpillar needs a cocoon to create stability while massive changes occur. You can use the four elements as your cocoon, as your new home, while you dismantle the old."

"Use the Four Elements of Change as a path back to your true self, which is neither young nor old, but eternal," one of the elders continues, opening his arms wide. "Come into balance with the four elements of life. Each element represents a part of your being. When you bring the four elements into harmony, you will be in alignment with your center."

"Use these elements to support you while you dismantle the structure that keeps you trapped in fear," another elder says, stepping forward to take my hands in hers. "Then spread this message. Let the power of your new knowing emanate like warm rays of light to help others find their center. We can only make great change in the world when we are centered within ourselves."

The elders bless me and slowly dissolve. I stand alone in the meadow, embodying the qualities of air, fire, water, and earth. Taking a calm, full breath, I gaze at the vastness of the sky and smile.

The Four Elements of Change

The dream of the elders illustrates how the elements of air, fire, water, and earth can be allies on our path of transformation. As you recreate yourself, these four elements become the building blocks of a new foundation. Each element represents a part of your being. When you integrate all four elements, you balance all parts of yourself and naturally live from your center.

Each of the elements has a complementary action—an art—for you to learn. We begin with air, but working with the four elements is not a linear process. The elements and their actions blend and support one another to create a container for change.

Air represents the mental body. The action of air is to clearly see.

The first element of change focuses on the art of clear perception. The journey to center is greatly sped up by a compassionate and supportive mind. Since you have probably spent much time in fear-based or judgmental thinking, the mind is probably one of the most difficult aspects of self to change. With patience and practice and a conscious shift in attitude, you can move from the heaviness of a fearful, disruptive mind to the lightness of a clear, supportive mind.

Fire represents the energetic body. The action of fire is to clean.

Fire represents your spirit and the energetic aspect of your being. The second element in your new structure, fire, will teach you about the power of cleaning. The fire element is about action. After you witness through the eyes of air, you move into cleaning out what is no longer true. Cleaning is not something you do just once in your life, then it's over. Action, just like learning to walk, is about repetition and practice.

Water represents the emotional body. The action of water is to open.

The gift of water is learning to open yourself to all things. It is easy to stay open to things you like or that feel good; it's more difficult to stay open to things you dislike or that feel bad. To open means accepting all that life brings while simultaneously choosing to work for positive change. Opening is not a passive, discouraged acceptance of your inner world or outer reality. It is a courageous internal movement of trust into the new life that is unfolding.

Earth represents the physical body. The action of earth is to nourish.

The final element in your circle is earth. Earth represents the physical body and the importance of nourishing yourself from the inside out. Self-nourishment is about learning what actions (from what you eat to how many hours you sleep to whom you spend time with) deplete you and which vitalize you. When you feed your center consciously, you will support your physical body in being as vibrant and healthy as possible.

As you read the following chapters, each dedicated to one element, choose one or more of the corresponding practice exercises that feel most relevant to you. These exercises will help you integrate the qualities of each element into your daily life. At the very end of each chapter, I also share a way to nonverbally anchor yourself in the wisdom of the four elements by building a personal altar that honors the individual qualities of air, fire, water, and earth.

The final chapter in *The Toltec Path of Transformation,* The Fifth Element: Beyond Structure, explores how, once you embody the four elements, you can step beyond your structure completely and into the fifth element, your divine center.

3

Air:
The Art of Clear Perception

Regaining Your Clarity and Vision

When the doors of perception are
cleansed, man will see things as they truly
are, infinite.

—William Blake

While there are many different perspectives on how to walk a Toltec path, there is one common denominator in all Toltec teachings: the importance of awareness. Nowhere in our being is the practice of awareness more important than in our relationship with our mind.

Modern society highly values the mind, often to the exclusion of the other aspects of self: spiritual, emotional, and physical. When the mind is out of balance with the rest of your being, fear results. At times of change, instead of going within to tap into the resources of spirit, emotions, and body, the mind grasps at external validation, substances, and people to feel stable and supported. Whatever you find outside yourself to help you feel whole and stable, whether it is a relationship, a job, or your youth, it can only bring a temporary sense of security, since it may be taken away at any time. This leads to a life overflowing with worry and stress.

In this incredible time of change in social, economic, political, and personal structures, learning how to shift your mental attention from fear and dread to clarity, trust, and possibility, regardless of what changes are happening around you, is vital. The world is changing too quickly for you to rest in the past or the familiar stabilizing forces of your job, relationship, or home. It is time to tap a deeper sense of faith and cultivate a mind that supports your growth and the unfolding of your greatest potential.

One way your thoughts are particularly unhelpful during times of change is anytime you weave together exaggerated scenarios of scarcity and danger. I call this "disaster mind." Also known as worst-case scenario and negative mind, disaster mind is constantly scanning for what could go wrong. When something does go wrong, disaster mind only makes it worse. It thrives on judgment, comparison, fear, and scarcity. When you see through the eyes of disaster mind, you often bounce between the past and the future, rarely showing up in the present moment, which is the only place true transformation can happen.

The first element of change is the art of clear perception. Your path of transformation is greatly sped up by a compassionate and present mind. Imagine what it would be like to have a supportive, creative mind when challenges arise! But changing the workings of your mind isn't easy. It will require patience and practice and a conscious shift in attitude, but moving from fearful mind to clear mind is possible.

The Mind in Action

Many years ago, I experienced the incredible chaos that the mind can create when I decided to be in silence for forty days for Lent. My intent for going into silence was to connect more deeply with my center. I wanted to give myself time off from interacting verbally and focus on my own inner sense of peace.

The first few days of silence were wonderful. But silence and I had a short honeymoon. The next two weeks were perfect hell. Perfect, because what arose was exactly what I needed to see. My extended silence gave me the gap I'd needed to see the workings of my mind in action. During this time, I gave my mind a new nickname: disaster mind, because of the immense drama and judgment that was present in my mind for much of the time.

Here's my story of meeting and transforming my disaster mind.

When I first began my silence, I lived in a tiny cabin in the woods, forty-five minutes outside town. The road to work was winding and steep and ran along a deep river ravine.

As I drove to town one morning, I was startled by the loudness of my mind. "You are late for work!" it screamed at me. "You are going to get fired!" Then my mind created a whole inner movie for me to watch: getting fired, losing my house, losing all my friends, and ending up destitute.

When that vision ran to its bitter end, another one started. "You are going too fast; you are going to go over the edge of the road!" I envisioned myself running through the guardrail and plunging over the edge to the river below. I saw myself dying or, even worse, being trapped in the car, still alive but badly mangled and with no one to help me.

"What is my mind doing?" I asked myself. I felt split in two: One part of me was watching a completely separate part of me as it created chaos with words and images.

As the disaster scenarios of my mind unfolded one after another, and the voices of fear proved impossible to ignore, I was shocked. A bigger shock occurred when I realized that the disaster voices had always been there, chattering away. My silence had not created them but had allowed me to quiet down enough so that I could hear what was previously below my consciousness. This was the key to learning how to shift my mind from disaster to clarity.

My silence forced me to simply witness my thoughts and my reaction to them. I noticed that when I paid attention to my disaster thoughts, they got louder, as if they knew they had an audience. One moment, I would be comparing myself to someone else and making up a story about how I was failing. The next moment, my mind was judging the very person I had compared myself to. I started losing faith that my mind always acted in my best interest. If I weren't being aware, I believed what my mind was telling me. As I became more conscious of the dramas, I could see the thoughts were not the truth.

Over the next few weeks, I practiced witnessing with compassion, rather than being caught by the fear and worry of my own mind. When I put my attention elsewhere, the voices lessened in intensity.

Witnessing the voices without giving them any extra energy (they had plenty on their own, thank you!) taught me many things about my mind. When you witness your own perceptions, you harness a great force for change. When you become conscious of the mind's stories and witness them objectively, you are empowered to consciously choose what you want to believe, instead of running on automatic pilot. At first it may be painful to see the fullness of your mind's chaos. But the recognition of what is not working will lead you to "change" your mind and give it new guidelines.

And there is another reward waiting for you when you shift your disaster mind. As I stopped believing my disaster mind, I noticed another voice that spoke to me all the time. It was a quiet, sweet voice that was easily drowned out by negative thinking. When I allowed the negative thinking to pass on through, this voice remained.

The first time I heard this sweet, compassionate voice, it startled me. I was rushing to get to work and realized I had forgotten something. "Oops, let's go back and get it!" a laughing voice said in my head. I looked around, confused. Where was my judge? Where was the familiar voice that told me how bad I was? This new voice connected me with my intuition and with a great sense of love and acceptance of everyone around me—and for myself.

Here's how you, too, can release disaster mind and find the loving voice within.

Seeing Your Own Disaster Mind

By playing a simple game, you can begin to see the nature of your own mind.

To play this game, spend your morning commute (or set aside half an hour during your day) noticing your thoughts. Pretend that you are listening to a radio station and are curious about the program. Keep breathing as you listen! Your goal is to practice *witnessing* your thoughts, not believing them.

Allow yourself to really hear your disaster mind, and be present with it. Notice where it is making up stories, freaking out about something that has not come to pass, or looking at the past for what things might go wrong in the future.

The mind gets stuck in thinking it sees reality, when it is really only looking through veils of mistaken agreements. Disaster mind, a mind tangled in old agreements, cannot see what is real. Going back to our example in chapter 1, if you make the agreement that "Mom loves my brother more than me," you will believe it fully, no matter how much evidence there is that your mom, in fact, loves you very much. Then disaster mind takes this agreement and tangles it up even further: "Mom doesn't love me. No one loves me. I am unlovable." What you end up with is a very messy mind, perceiving all sorts of unrealities and believing they are true.

Even when there is an actual disaster in your life, you still don't need the guidance of your disaster mind; you need the help of your own clarity. Believing disaster thoughts such as, "Losing my job and home means my life is over" or "I'll never love again after this terrible divorce," drain your energy and close all the doors to possibility. A healthy mind looks for the potential and the promise of growth through adversity.

One of my students wrote to me after she was abruptly and unjustly fired from her job. Terry wanted support, because she could see the power of her disaster mind, and she was ready to do something different with this transition in her life. She wrote, "I'm really wanting to move with integrity and ease into a new environment that feels more in line with my gifts and interests." Terry was guiding her mind to the truth of what was now possible and asking for help to not dwell on the storm-cloud thoughts of injustice. From a place of clarity, she had scheduled to talk to a lawyer. She modeled beautifully, taking actions from clear mind and the importance of asking for reminders and guidance to stay off the familiar road of disaster mind to remain on the path of aware choices.

To truly support yourself, learn to look closely at how you motivate or defeat yourself with every step. The rest of this chapter will give you the tools to move out of disaster thinking and into compassionate clarity and connect to the part of your mind that will sweet talk you through any transition.

Stopping Disaster Mind in Its Tracks

judging others?

Proper grammar is a great strategy for disarming the might of disaster mind. Like most of us, you probably have a tendency to create huge run-on sentences of judgment upon judgment. Once you learn why it's not helpful to judge yourself, you can discover that when you are judging yourself, you get disappointed, angry, or ashamed. You then link your judgments to how others may be judging you or compare yourself with others.

"These pants don't fit me very well; my thighs are too fat; oh, if only I had the willpower to stop eating so much sugar then my thighs and butt wouldn't be so big; and if only I worked out more, like Christy, my body would be okay like hers; her body is so beautiful, and mine is so ugly that no one is going to want to date me, so why am I even bothering to try on new pants; they are not going to hide the fact that I am ugly, and that no one loves me, that I am all alone and am never going to be appreciated for who I am, because I live in a society that judges people who are bigger than a size 4, and I was never a size 4, no matter how much I dieted, though maybe if I was better at dieting my thighs wouldn't be so big, and I wouldn't be so unhappy all the time . . ."

When you catch yourself judging yourself for judging yourself or comparing yourself with others, put a period in the sentence at the first opportunity. "These pants don't fit me." Period. Now create a new sentence, a new paragraph, which supports you with a new thought: "My thighs are the thighs of a grown woman, not the thighs of a teenager." Or "I am looking forward to working out and getting my body in shape." Notice if you judged yourself, and notice how it affected you. "Ah, I just judged myself for having fat thighs and ended up hating myself." Now bring in the kind hands of a parent encouraging a child to take another step. Shift your perspective away from judging yourself and toward acceptance and presence.

Here is another example of how you can use clear perception and proper punctuation to bring clarity and ease to a difficult situation. My friend Fred recently lost his job. He went back to work at his former job in the interim, with plans to start teaching and getting his own business going. But frustrating roadblocks kept popping up. The person whom he was going to teach with kept backing out at the last minute. Another relative who was going to help him with his new class suddenly had to leave town for an extended business trip. The deadline he had given for himself to teach his first class and start his new career was looming. Each day, his stress level built and built as his disaster mind starting singing its song in his ears. We sat down to explore how to help him shift his state of mind and move things forward again.

My first question to him was: "What is your mind telling you?"

Together we sat in witness as he gave his disaster mind voice: "I want to start my new business, and I had people who were going to help me but keep flaking out, so I'm never going to be able to get my new business going; no one will help me, no one follows through; I try and try and nothing is working out right; I'm doomed to continue to do the same work, even though my body is failing me, and I probably can't do it for too much longer, and my mom is not doing well, and what if she is really sick, and I can't take care of her; how am I going to manage, and my car needs to be fixed, and I don't have the money . . ."

As he was speaking, he realized that all he was seeing were the negative aspects of his situation, and that his disaster mind was weaving in lots of fears that were making him feel even more hopeless and paralyzed. I invited him to take a mental step back and place a period in his sentence: "I want to start my new business."

"Now what other possibilities do you see?" I asked him.

"I put an unrealistic deadline on myself, and it is making me crazy and locking me into the thinking that there is only one thing to do next. When I see from clarity, there are many other people I can talk to who might be able to help me in my goals. I really want to start my own business, and need to look for where the openings are, rather than focusing on the closed doors. I need to be more patient with the process and not put so much pressure on myself or other people. Now I'm feeling excited again!"

The clarity my friend found by putting a period in his disaster thinking and starting a new sentence from awareness was profound. But one moment of awareness is not enough; to anchor to a new way of seeing the world, especially in tough situations, we have to diligently shift our perspective away from disaster mind and toward clear perception—over and over again.

With your eyes, you shift your perspective thousands of times a day. Raise a finger about four inches in front of your eyes and focus on it completely. Now shift your focus to something in the distance. Notice how your finger is still there, but it is only a tiny part of a much bigger framework. You can do the same perspective shift with your disaster-creating, judging mind as you move into your witnessing mind.

Making the Transition to Clear Perception

Each of us, as individuals, as communities, and on a global level, is in a period of transition. Whether you are learning a new skill for your job, working to release an old belief you have uncovered, starting a new romance, recovering from an addiction, or choosing to take care of your body in a new way, learning to use the mind in a supportive role will ease any change. When you are trapped in disaster mind, it is as if the house of your being is being buffeted by a tornado. You cower in the basement or rage at the storm.

When you calm your disaster mind, mental chaos dissolves into a clarifying spring breeze that blows away the dust and cobwebs so that you can clearly see what your next step is. Calling on the element of air and the art of clear perception provides the support you need to bring into your life the following scaffolding:

patience

love

compassion

acceptance

a "You can do it!" attitude

a safe space

encouragement

humor

Remember that during the shift from disaster mind to positive mind, you will need tremendous patience, humor, and encouragement. Whenever a negative, detrimental thought arises, simply witness it. Do your best to not judge yourself. Notice what happens when you think negatively. How does your body feel? Where does your mind take you when it goes into fear?

As you practice learning to witness your mind with love, acceptance, and a laugh, you can more easily see and avoid the three main pitfalls of your disaster mind: judgment, perfectionism, and unbalanced responsibility.

Pitfall #1: Judgment

The judge—our negative mind—sees things in terms of black and white. Instead of simply being aware that a certain plant will make you sick if you eat it, the judge says, "That plant is bad," simplifying and judging a plant that may be beneficial in other circumstances.

Using the witness, you can train yourself to stop listening to the judge as your main source of information. You can open your vision to include all the resources in your being. When you truly witness this vast sky of the mind, you will find silence and peace. You will be conscious of the stormy thoughts below, but your attention will remain fixed on the expansiveness of your awareness, not on the endless dramas of your disaster mind. When you learn to rest the mind in this place of soft witnessing, the judge dissolves like mist into a flow of acceptance.

Below are examples of judging mind versus witnessing mind:

Judge: That person is bad.

Witness: *I do not feel comfortable around that person.*

Judge: I am worthless and undesirable.

Witness: *I am feeling vulnerable and weak today.*

Judge: I keep judging and fighting with my boss. She makes me feel like a terrible person. She is unreasonable and uncaring.

Witness: *I need to stay out of my boss's way when she is angry, or I tend to get angry myself and make things worse. Her moods do not have anything to do with me. She seems to get angry most often in the mornings. I will practice being kind.*

Judge: My thighs are fat. I'm never going to find someone to love me.

Witness: *I'm not happy with my body right now. Am I comparing myself to how I think I should be? Am I making up stories about what others will think?*

By cultivating the witness, you learn to allow what is. By allowing what is, you naturally step into acceptance. When acceptance motivates your actions, you forgive yourself for your perceived faults and imperfections. Your choices are guided by love. They come from a wider perception of body, emotions, and a life force in balance with the tool of the mind.

As your perception clears, you become your own loving parent, your own best friend and mentor. You become the artist of your own life. You can now create a new framework from which to live and breathe—a fresh structure in which you can maintain your center.

Pitfall #2: Perfectionism

Do you try to be perfect in everything you do? Do you try to not make mistakes so that you can avoid the punishment you dole out to yourself? You need a safe space as you dismantle your old structure. Punishing yourself with pointed words and stabs does not help your internal remodeling. It is an illusion that punishing yourself will make you a better person or will stop you from making wrong choices. Learning from your experiences with curious eyes is what fosters the fastest growth.

Stop for a moment to explore what it feels like to try to never make a mistake. When you spend your energy trying not to make mistakes, your way of life becomes stilted and tight. You constantly look around to see if anyone is watching. You feel that to be adequate, you must be perfect.

Your mind is always ready to tell you how you are doing everything wrong, and it constantly judges and compares you with others: "See, they never make mistakes."

This sort of perfectionism is a horrible way to live. If you expect yourself to be perfect at everything you do, you will stifle your creativity and sense of adventure. All sense of fun and spontaneity disappears. To deconstruct any detrimental perfectionism in yourself, start by consciously celebrating your mistakes. Invite yourself to honor your imperfections. Soon you will see that they are not imperfections after all, but are a part of the wholeness of a growing, maturing being.

I am a recovering perfectionist. Without awareness of my behaviors, I strove to be perfect in every way. I judged myself for every mistake. I worried that others would see I was not always perfect. I compared myself to people I thought were perfect. My friend Gini continued to point out to me the toll my need to be perfect was having on me. She started teasing me whenever I tried to be perfect. Gradually, I learned to tease myself.

One day, during a journey to the pyramids in Teotihuacan, Mexico, I invited a group of students to share their worst-case scenarios—what their disaster mind told them was the truth. "No one is ever going to love me. I am unlovable." "I am broken. No matter how much I want to heal, I never will." "I am never going to be good enough." "If I am not perfect, no one will like me."

We agreed to tease each other for the rest of the day based on these disaster-mind fears.

"I know I am not perfect, and you are never going to like me, but can I walk with you?"

"Well, I am broken, and I am never going to heal, so I guess it is okay to be with someone imperfect like you."

"I knew it! I am never going to be good enough to climb the pyramid. You all are so much stronger than I am. I can't do it."

"You are right; you're not good enough. But will you love me if I help you climb?"

It was incredibly freeing to clearly see and admit what our fears were and to make fun of them.

Honesty and humor are amazing antidotes for the disease of disaster mind. When you laugh at your own mind and find it silly, it loses its ferocious power. As the mind surrenders to supporting your whole being rather than being right about its old agreements, clarity emerges. Awareness allows you to uncover the unconscious agreements that take you away from center. You learn to discern the truth, rather than judge what you don't like.

To release the grip of perfectionism, practice praising yourself instead of punishing yourself when you make a mistake. Lovingly tease yourself for your striving, and remind yourself over and over again that the goal isn't to be perfect; the goal is to be whole.

Pitfall #3: Unbalanced Responsibility

Another way you might get stuck on your path is by being irresponsible or by being overly responsible. Responsibility is tricky. You can stunt your own growth in two ways: by asking other people to carry you or by trying to constantly carrying others. Pay attention to the situations in which you do not take responsibility for your own journey, but also notice the flip side—the situations in which you take responsibility for someone else's journey.

Trust that when others fall down, they will figure out how to get themselves up again. You can always lend a hand, but sometimes the hand you lend is actually what is keeping them down. Share with them all of your love, support, faith, encouragement. But keep your focus on your own journey, on picking yourself up with love and faith and letting others do the same for themselves.

Giving others the space to find their own feet is not easy. I experienced the importance of putting faith in other people's ability to take self-responsibility from one of my students when I lived in Berkeley, California.

Robert walked into the Toltec Center seeking community. He had recently moved from Arizona to California. For the first six months that I knew him, he struggled to find a place to live, to secure a job he liked, and to manage his finances. At first we were all happy to support his new life in Berkeley. He borrowed money from several different people and slept on many couches. I let him take many classes for free or for work in trade.

His life continued to be chaotic. He constantly found and lost housing and jobs. After months of no real improvement, I inquired into his background. He owed many people money in Arizona and had basically tapped out his resources in his former community.

I called him, and we had a long talk about personal responsibility and the importance of creating stability for himself. I pointed out that we had supported him as best we could, but I now believed we were disempowering him by catching him every time he fell. I knew it would be hard, but we both agreed it was time for him to learn to catch himself.

Our community made an agreement to stop loaning him money. We encouraged him to focus completely on his physical foundation—to find a good living situation and a job that supported him.

It was challenging for me personally to tell him no. Each time Robert asked to borrow money, I invited him to rely on his own resources. At one point, he ended up in a homeless shelter, then lived in transitional housing. My judging mind kept telling me that I should feel guilty for not helping someone when I had the resources to do so, that I was hurting Robert, that I was a bad person. I kept focusing on my greater desire to support Robert in a new way, to help him to take responsibility for his life.

Despite my fearful thoughts, I was able to consciously witness my mind throughout this process. This allowed me to stay open to Robert. I encouraged him to recreate his life by choosing a job he felt comfortable with and, as his spiritual practice, to put all his attention on keeping that job. Our community holding him in this new way helped Robert to realize that simply taking care of himself was his path of transformation. He found a stable job and eventually located housing that he could afford and that nurtured him. He later thanked me for my support and faith in him, which, as he said, "Was what I needed to take responsibility for my life and stop believing that I would only make it if other people saved me."

And the gift for many in our community was holding a clear vision of the possibility of change for Robert while not caretaking him. Today Robert is working at a job he loves, is doing his photography, and is living his dream as an artist of his life rather than a victim of circumstances.

As you step beyond the mental pitfalls of judgment, perfectionism, and unbalanced responsibility, you will begin to tap the well of creativity within your mind. When your mind no longer believes it needs to control you or anyone else, it will relax and do its actual job: visioning and manifesting the life you want to live.

Becoming the Artist of Your Life

When you judge, try to be perfect, or are overly responsible or irresponsible, you negatively polarize what you perceive and do not leave space for love and gratitude. A beautiful Chinese saying reminds me of the power of being in the present moment with a mind as clear as a bell: "Now that my barn has burned to the ground, I can more easily see the moon."

To shift your perception, consciously become an artist, an architect of love. Artists can look at a rundown shack and see beyond the debris to the gem within. A true artist does not ignore what is and fantasize only about what could be, but recognizes and is excited about the work ahead.

With clear perception, you can witness, with a curious eye, your mind and all the circumstances of your life as a wonderful remodeling project in progress. Curiosity and a good dose of humor are the best antidotes for overhauling the serious, self-absorbed, modern mind. The art of seeing with new eyes will allow you to simply look at the limiting structure of your being and responses to change without drama or struggle.

You are a work in progress. You have been trained to live outside your center. Wherever you are on your journey inward, be compassionate. Every time you judge or compare yourself to others, you are taking a step backward. Watch for it, but be kind to yourself about it, too. Remember your choice to be an artist who creates, rather than a critic who destroys.

With your perception, you can use what you see to hurt or heal. Therefore, getting your perception in alignment is a high priority. Again, this takes time and patience and plenty of falling down and getting up. Be gentle and persistent with yourself. All of the elements and their gifts will guide you to clearer perception. As you embody each of them, you will learn the art of moving yourself toward healing, rather than toward further mental or emotional suffering.

The next element in our circle, fire, will teach you how to clean and clear out the old agreements that block your inner magic.

Practices

Mind Exploration

Spend a week noticing how you perceive yourself. What eyes do you use to watch yourself? If you were a child learning to walk, what would you be saying to yourself? Keep a record of your perceptions. You can use index cards or a little notebook or even a tape recorder to record impressions in the moment. Do your best to witness, to be an explorer looking at new, interesting terrain. There is nothing you need to do or change this week. You are gathering information.

If you find you are judging yourself for your perceptions, remember grammar and punctuation: "Period!" Stop any run-on sentences emanating from your judging self. Pretend you are witnessing the mind of your dearest, most beloved friend. Bring all of your compassion and clarity to this task.

On a piece of paper, make three columns: perception, based on, and rewrite. In the first column, take quick notes of what you perceive without thinking about or analyzing them:

"I am going to be late for work. I am bad."

"I hate my hair."

"I look old."

"I am excited about my date tonight."

"What if he doesn't like me?"

"I'm tired of this job."

"Maria is selfish and uncaring."

"I am angry at myself for not standing up for myself."

"I wish I were more like Brian."

"I'm afraid of losing my job and my home."

At the end of each day, go back over your notes and mark in the second column which comments support you and take you toward your center and which are *based on* fear, judgment, comparison, feeling victimized, and so on. Note if you see core agreements that might stem from old childhood beliefs. What are you really saying to yourself?

Go through your entire list; in the third column, rewrite your perception, imagining you are teaching yourself to walk. You might find that you write the exact same words, but the energy of the words is very different. Can you discern and support rather than judge? Take responsibility for how you feel.

PERCEPTION	BASED ON	REWRITE
"I am going to be late for work. I am bad."	Fear, core agreement	I did not leave myself enough time to get ready. Tomorrow I will set my alarm earlier so I do not have to rush.
"I hate my hair."	Comparison	My hair is curlier than usual today.
"I look old."	Comparison	My skin is changing.
"I am excited about my date tonight."	Center	
"What if he doesn't like me?"	Fear, core agreement	I wonder if we will get along?
"I am tired of this job."	Judgment or, perhaps, motivation	How can I bring more excitement to this job?
"Maria is selfish and uncaring."	Judgment	My stomach knots up when Maria is curt.
"I am angry at myself for not standing up for myself."	Victimized	I feel small and powerless, and then I get angry at myself when I don't speak my truth.
"I wish I were more like Brian."	Comparison	I like Brian's honesty.
"I am afraid of losing my job and home."	Fear	I honor my fears and open to new possibilities on how to maintain my job and home.

Remember, this is an exercise to track old beliefs and current ways of thinking. It is not a means by which to judge yourself for your judgments! It is a way for you to look at your mind and notice where you can shift your perception. You can use this exercise to make yourself suffer more, by judging yourself, or you can use it as an exploration of disaster mind. Please do your best to witness and be curious, rather than attacking yourself further!

Showing Up in This Moment

Another way we can clear our perception is by coming into the present moment. To explore what your mind is up to, spend fifteen minutes sitting quietly, watching your thoughts. Get a new piece of paper and make three columns. Mark them past, present, and future. Close your eyes, and let your mind go. Notice your thoughts. When a thought about the past arises, make a mark in the "past" column. When you are in the present, make a mark in the "present" column. When you find yourself in the future, make a mark in the "future" column.

When you are done, count up the marks in each column and put a total for each at the bottom. Do this exercise once a week for a month: see if you can begin to train your mind to stay more in the present. This takes practice and encouragement. Remember, your mind is learning to walk in the present. Support yourself in this new skill. Be a loving parent to yourself. Here are examples of past, present, and future thinking:

PAST	PRESENT	FUTURE
I forgot to buy mayonnaise.	It is warm in this room.	I wonder what Fred will do if he gets the job he wants?
A memory of being betrayed by your best friend when you were twelve	Appreciating your breath	Dreaming about what you will say on your next date with George
I wonder if I did that project correctly.	I am grateful to have finished my project.	Will I get a raise if the project I completed is well received?
Replaying a past discussion over and over in your head	I did the best I could in my talk with Liz.	Liz is going to misinterpret what I said and tell her friends.

Media Fast

One way to clear your mind is to change the input you are giving it. The various media reflect and nourish the fear and scarcity aspects of your mind and cloud your vision. They reflect how our culture reinforces looking outside ourselves for a sense of inner balance. When was the last time you saw an ad that read something like this? "You are perfect exactly as you are. Would you like to buy our shampoo?" Most advertising is based on the premise of lack: "If you drink our beer, you will have the charisma you have always wanted" or "This car will give you the prestige and recognition you are looking for." The message over and over is: "You are not enough as you are, but if you just buy this gizmo, everything will be okay."

The news media also give us insight into why our minds love to worry. In newspapers and on television news, we are repetitively shown examples of war, murder, poverty, and instability in the world. The truth is, millions of different things are happening simultaneously around the world. Can you imagine picking up a major newspaper with a top headline reading "Woman Reaches Enlightenment, full story on page 2"? Imagine how different the world could be if we gave as much emphasis to spiritual development and joyous events in the media as we currently give to fear-based events.

For a day or a week, do a media fast. You might choose to stop watching television for a day or refrain from watching the news or reading magazines or newspapers for a week. Instead, tap into sites, such as goodnews.com, that celebrate change and creativity. Notice how you feel after your media fast.

Connecting to the Element of Air

The shift from disaster mind to clear perception is made up of a million little acts of awareness, combined with the action of shifting your focus over and over again. Consciously connecting with the element of air will support you in making this shift.

Start by going through your home and opening every window. Invite the wind to blow in and clear out any old habitual perceptions and cyclical thoughts. As you open each window, say out loud what you would like to shift in your perception. Here are some examples:

"I invite the wind in to blow away my fears about the future and to remind me to slow down and come back to enjoying the present moment."

"As I open this window, I open to a new perspective in my life."

"May the winds of change breathe new vision into my life. I release my judgmental thoughts and invite clarity."

You can repeat one sentence over and over again at each window, or you can say something different each time. You might even write down your sentences and tape them to one or more window sills, so that in the future, each time you open the window, you are reminded of your new perception.

As you do this practice, keep your awareness in this moment and feel the wind moving through your house. Invite the wind to move through all the rooms, bringing fresh perspectives and blowing away any confusion, lack of vision, or tangled thoughts.

Stand in the middle of your home and breathe this fresh air into your being. Use your own connection to air, your breath, to release any stuck thoughts, and bring yourself into the present moment. Intentionally breathe more clarity and space into your mind and body.

In the future, when you are feeling muddled or confused, go back to this feeling of the wind against your skin. Imagine opening a window inside your being and letting the air blow away the fear and judgments of disaster mind.

Inner Guidance

Air Visualization for Creating a New Container

Visualization is a great technique to help you create new pathways in the mind and body. When we visualize something in our minds, we energize it and make it real. We call on invisible forces to support and guide us. For centuries, shamans have used visualization and spiritual journeying to connect with allies and gain information.

This visualization is a powerful way to bring the teachings from the Dream of the Elders into your own life. To help create your new structure, you can call in a guardian from each of the four elements to remind you of the new qualities you are embodying.

The first guardian is from the element of air. From air **you learn the art of clear perception—the right use of your mind.**

1. Make your body comfortable and take some deep breaths into your belly.

2. Imagine yourself standing in the middle of a beautiful stone circle. This circle encompasses and holds all of you in its embrace. Facing one direction, ask for guidance and vision from the element of air to help you perceive yourself clearly.

3. Invite an air guide to join you and help you see with new eyes. Be open to how that guide may appear. Your air guide may be an animal, a person you know, or a stranger. It may be a quiet voice in your head or a knowing in your body. Your guardian of air may not come to you immediately, but later in a dream or while you are in the middle of your day, this guide may appear. The wind may come to whisper in your ear. Pray for the seeds of a new structure to sprout, so that you may feel

supported as you dissolve your old ways of seeing and being.

4. When you feel complete, ask for a symbol to represent this new anchor, and imagine it marking one direction of your circle.

To further support yourself, you can build an altar to represent your journey. Choose an object to represent your centered self and surround it with stones or beads or objects to represent your circle of acceptance for what is. As you call in each of your guardians, pick an object to represent this guardian and place it outside the circle. A feather or a pair of glasses or any object that pleases you can represent air and your new vision. Set your intent to use all of the elements and their gifts to guide you through your fears and old beliefs, through disaster mind, and back to your center.

4

Fire:
The Art of Cleaning

Clearing What No Longer Serves You

All the means of action—the shapeless masses—the materials—lie everywhere about us. What we need is the celestial fire to change the flint into the transparent crystal, bright and clear. That fire is genius.

—Henry Wadsworth Longfellow

Fire represents our spirit and the energetic aspect of our being. As the second element in our circle, fire teaches us about the wisdom of cleaning.

Although the "how" may be explained differently, the importance of clearing your perception and cleaning unwanted structures is shared by all spiritual and psychological paths. We may start the journey of cleaning our inner home in either a hopeful or desperate state, but often we are surprised by the amount of old debris we have to navigate. Sometimes, we sabotage ourselves when any real change begins to take place. This chapter will teach you how to raise the energy needed to thoroughly— top to bottom—cleanse and purify your energetic body.

For the Toltec, each human is a specific ray of light, an individual vibration of energy. This light, or energy, is the unique essence of who you are. Your physical body is the visible part of your being. Your energetic body is the invisible part that flows through and around your physical body. Your energetic body communicates with and receives information from a variety of sources. It shares this information with your mental, emotional, and physical bodies.

Agreements, especially the unconscious agreements you made as a child, clutter your energetic body and bog you down. When you make an agreement, it eventually becomes a static structure in your energetic body that saps your vitality. These structures can cause you to perceive the world in ways that reinforce your beliefs. They also cause confusion among your energetic, mental, emotional, and physical bodies.

When I first started investigating my thoughts, I was horrified by what I found. Here I was, a supposedly spiritual person, with heaps of judgment, fear, and stagnant beliefs in my unconscious. I spent a great deal of time judging myself before I accomplished any actual cleaning. Eventually, I saw that any time I spent judging myself was like tracking mud all over my house while complaining loudly about the dirt. Having clear perception allowed me to take off my muddy shoes first, then investigate what I wanted to keep in my house and what I wanted to clear away.

Opening the Door to Cleaning

Imagine yourself as a house that you keep fairly clean for the outside world. By keeping your house clean, you get approval and acceptance from the outside world. Every house has a closet, and into yours you stuff everything that you do not like about yourself: all the unconscious agreements, inner voices, and behaviors that have been passed down to you from your family.

When you invite people over, you are friendly, until they get anywhere near your closet. "Don't open that!" you say with a threatening look. You do not want anyone to see what lurks behind the closed doors.

Or maybe you are a person who invites others over and immediately drags them to your closet. "Look at all of this! Can you believe it? It is so awful!" Comparing what's in your overflowing closet to other people's has now become a hobby.

In either case, one day you decide it is time to clean out your inner closet. Maybe you read a book that says it is a good idea. Maybe you are in so much pain, you are willing to do anything to feel better.

The question is: If you are really going to clean out a closet, what do you need?

The first step to successful closet cleaning is your own willingness. It is not enough to think cleaning is a good idea; you must have desire and commitment to go the distance. Otherwise you will not bring all of your resources to the task. Willingness comes when you clearly perceive the truth about how your old structures are causing you to suffer. Once you stop blaming others (and this includes not blaming yourself!), you see clearly that it is *your* thoughts behind *your* actions and reactions that are at the root of the problem. This is actually a great relief, because the only thing you can truly change is you.

Willingness doesn't mean that you know exactly what and how to clean; it means that you are ready to explore and learn as you go along. Which brings us to our second step in the art of cleaning.

Once you harness the power of your willingness, it is time to pull everything out of the closet so that you can see what is inside.

This is where many people stumble.

What happens to your nice, clean, presentable house when you pull everything out of that musty back closet? Everything that was hidden and tucked neatly away is suddenly out in the open, strewn all over the rooms of your life. What seemed like a really good idea—pulling everything out of the closet—is now majorly messing up your house.

You might get overwhelmed. You might blame others. You might tell yourself, "See, I am really messed up. No one else could possibly have this much stuff." Suddenly, the path you are on is wrong, your teacher is no good, or you are beyond all possible hope. Your reaction to this new, very obvious mess might be to look around and say, "Okay, this is not working!" The temptation is to immediately shove everything back into the closet and shut the door.

This is why clear perception is so crucial. If you open the doors to untangle your structure, and your perception is still trapped in disaster mind, all you will be able to see is the chaos. Instead of cleaning, you will judge what is inside and end up creating even more dirt.

When you choose to truly clean out what no longer serves you, you will open the door on some not-so-pleasant thoughts, emotions, and bodily sensations—ones that you have experienced in the past but stashed away. You will sometimes feel out of control, be unclear about what is yours and what is not, and be confused. This is all a natural part of dismantling old structures and cleaning up what doesn't work. The best attitude to take while tackling your inner closet is to be curious about what is inside and willing to sift through the garbage to find the truth.

When your mind is clear, you can look on the chaos with a sense of humor: "Wow, that is in my closet?"

Instead of becoming depressed at the piles of behaviors you have pulled into the light, you are excited to reclaim what is real and leave the rest behind.

Pulling everything out of your closet allows choice. Your clear mind keeps you from judging what you find. To be even more accurate, your clear mind notices what you judge and what you feel victimized by, without believing either. Everything that arises is a chance to dismantle your old structure.

When your thoughts are laid out in front of you, you can begin to sort through what belongs to you and what does not. Following the closet analogy, you will find old clothes that do not fit you anymore and old beliefs that do not serve you. You will find things others gave you that you never really liked, but you did not know how to refuse. You will find whole structures that were passed on from your ancestors. Cultivate a new attitude—"Check this out! What an interesting thing to believe!"—instead of "I am a failure. Look at this mess. It proves I am bad."

After a weekend workshop, William excitedly shared a beautiful example of internal closet clearing. "I've always felt I had to prove myself, which caused me a lot of stress and self-judgment. Today I realized I was holding a belief that wasn't mine. My father came from a poor family and believed that the only way to advance was to prove that he was smart. In his eyes, he never did succeed in the business world. I grew up believing I had to be smart, but I always felt that I wasn't. I see now that I have been carrying his belief that he wasn't smart, but it never belonged to me. I don't need to be smart or not smart; I just need to be me!"

Remember that you spent your entire lifetime building the structures that limit you. The remodeling process takes time and repeated intentional action. Sometimes it is necessary to bring in an expert closet wrangler to guide you through the places where you are stuck in your sorting and scrubbing and/or help you to find a community that will support you. Having support makes the work of cleaning much more enjoyable, and it goes more quickly.

The fire element is about action. After you witness through the eyes of air, you move into cleaning what is no longer true. Even if you are not sure exactly how it will happen, as you clean, your happiness, energy, and integrity will be uncovered. Just remember, cleaning is not something you do once in your life, then it is over. Action is about practice.

Beware the Gremlins!

One of the games I use to bring humor to the sometime intense work of cleaning is to personalize the forces that thwart change. I visualize them as small, green gremlins.

Gremlins are the guardians of your structure, and they will do anything to keep it intact. As you sort and clean your closet, gremlins will whisper and shout at you to distract you from your task. Gremlins can serve as your biggest allies, because they lead you where you want to go. When one of them shows up shouting, "Don't go that way!" or whispering words of fear in your ears, you know you are actually on the right track.

Here is a list of some different kinds of gremlins. As you clean your inner closet, keep an eye out for gremlins that disguise themselves as your friends. Listen to them, not for the truth they speak (for they're prone to lie), but for the information they reveal.

Fear: As you get closer to cleaning out big agreements and structures, the gremlins of fear will arise, shaking and moaning. Often these reveal you are on the right track. Fear gremlins appear real, but they are really more like smoke—easy to walk through once you get up the courage to do so. A fear gremlin might say, "You are never going to be good enough."

Defensiveness: When you are clean, there is nothing to prove; you just are. If you notice yourself defending a particular viewpoint or belief, pay attention. Often a gremlin is protecting its territory. The statement "I am right!" is a sure sign of this gremlin.

Not wanting to look bad: This is a corollary to defending. To not look bad, most of us tend to defend our actions. If you feel your image is at stake, or that you need to appear a certain way to gain approval or respect, pay attention. A gremlin is present. What is the agreement that is prompting your defensive action?

Sleepiness: As you clear out layers of debris and old agreements, you uncover the core foundations that keep you trapped. Gremlins will jump in and wave their wands in front of your eyes: "You are very sleepy. There is nothing here. Rest and forget everything." At such moments, rest may be fine, but keep your awareness intact so that when you wake up, you will get right back on track. A healthy amount of denial is okay at times. Go to a movie to escape your problem but not necessarily every night.

Huge emotions: Gremlins sometimes will get in and stir, stir, stir all your emotions. If you are having an emotional reaction that is out of proportion with the situation or appears out of nowhere, slow down and take a couple of deep breaths. Look beyond the current situation to earlier events.

Projecting onto others: This is a favorite gremlin tactic. It most often takes two forms. 1) You see and judge the things you do not like about yourself as being the traits of someone else; 2) you think that people outside you are seeing and judging all those things you hate about yourself. The gremlins are delighted when they can get you to project onto someone else or against yourself. For example, "My aunt thinks I am not smart enough to be a real success." In reality, your aunt might be supportive of you, but her support is veiled by the negative self-judgment that you project onto her because of her honesty in helping you identify your obstacle.

Compensating: This is what I call the pendulum tactic. One gremlin whispers, "You are too nice!" so you get mean. Later the gremlin whispers, "You are too mean!" When you are off center and heading back to balance, a gremlin will invite you to overcompensate, so that you become off balance in exactly the opposite way.

What other gremlins live in your closet?

Gremlins are actually fabulous help in your inner cleaning, as they mirror and guide you to the dirty spots. Thank the gremlins when they appear, instead of cursing them. Watching for your gremlins as you clean will prepare you for the next steps on your journey—short-term and long-term cleaning.

Two Types of Cleaning

One of the first times that I was aware of consciously cleaning my thoughts was in a bookstore in Berkeley.

It was a lazy day, and I was engaged in one of my favorite activities—browsing through books. I hung out in the self-help section, reading titles, enjoying the colors and texture of covers and paper, flipping through the books that looked interesting.

When I went to my car, I noticed that my energy level had plummeted. I felt bad without knowing why. I stopped everything and sat in my car, tracking what had happened.

Moving backward in time, I noticed how joyous I had been in the bookstore. As I witnessed more deeply, I saw myself in front of the self-help books and heard a voice that I had not noticed in the moment: "Look at all these books. All these people have been published. You are never going to write a book. And if you do, no one will read it. Everything has been written already. You don't have what it takes to write."

As I became quiet within myself, I made space for what was troubling me to arise and present itself. By bringing this voice into my conscious mind, I was able clean it out by not believing it. I knew that it was connected to deeper fears, but at that moment, all I needed to do was clear out that old thought and go on with my day. I told myself, "You will write many books because your heart wants to." My energy lifted, I felt happy again, and off I went.

In my mind, I made a little note. I had just done a short-term cleaning around the fear of not being published. Underneath this was a deeper fear, which I put in my long-term cleaning pile. This pile stemmed back to one big fear: not getting approval and, ultimately, not being loved.

I helped myself in two ways that day. The first way was by paying attention to my energy and clearing out a disaster mind thought. The second way was by witnessing that my fear of not being published was a larger part of my structure, related to needing outside validation.

Before tackling long-term cleaning, it helps to develop the skill of short-term cleaning. I was able to clear out my disaster mind thoughts and enjoy the rest of my day because of years of practice with short-term cleaning. Short-term cleaning includes the general pick-up, dusting, and washing of everyday life. Long-term cleaning entails larger renovations that take dedicated focus and space.

Short-Term Cleaning

Dirt obscures your center. When you physically clean, you remove the debris and clutter that hides the essence of the truth. Fear and self-doubt are clutter. They may arise as you make new choices. With every new action, you open a door within you. Behind that door lies not only your integrity but any fears you stashed there as a child.

When you picture your energetic structure as a house, you can see how the nooks and crannies can get dirty. When you are not looking, dust bunnies grow under the beds, and dirt piles up in unexpected places.

Short-term cleaning is about watching where you collect dirt in your system and each day clearing it out.

Imagine if you washed your dishes or your car one time and said, "Okay, I am done with that job. I never have to do it again." Or if you dusted your house one time, then became furious that it became dusty again. "How dare it get dusty again? I just dusted!" This sort of short-term cleaning can seem repetitive and trivial, but it is crucial.

One thing you can guarantee is that dirt happens. Both your physical world and your internal energetic world need daily cleaning and polishing. You know the importance of brushing your teeth daily, of washing your hands on a regular basis. Your energetic being is no different. It, too, accumulates dirt and grime from use.

Your energetic structure similarly snags energy in the rough places. If part of your old structure tells the story that "My mother doesn't love me," which has transformed into "I am not lovable," then each time you see the hint of an "I am not lovable" situation, it creates an emotional reaction within you; it snags you. You might see two people embracing and unconsciously think, "See, they have love, but I do not, because I am not lovable." The place within you that feels unlovable now has more dirt piled on top of it.

When dirt collects in your system, your energy decreases. You may find yourself thinking about something over and over again or feeling exhausted. This is the time to stop and check in with yourself: "Is there something I need to clean in this moment?"

Take the above incident. You see a couple embracing and you notice yourself starting to judge yourself for not being in a relationship. Or you are aware of feeling drained and tired, or you realize that you are angry. Take a moment to acknowledge what you are thinking or feeling, to witness what is going on for you.

Now, imagine disconnecting your experience from the couple's experience. You are having an experience based on your own dirt, not on their reality. Bless them, and take responsibility for the energy inside you.

Imagine cleaning out your energy. Your imagination is powerful. It can help to move and direct energy. You can use the image of a broom or of fire to cleanse and release whatever does not serve you in this moment. Any image will work. The more real you make the image, the more effective it will be.

Then invite a new thought to creatively shape what you do. Ask yourself, "What is the truth?" You may realize, "Oh, that's right; I am choosing not to be in a relationship right now!" or "I miss being intimate with someone. I am going to ask my best friend for a hug and to go for a walk with me."

As you continue to pay attention to your thoughts, you will learn about what type of dirt you tend to collect. Use this information to put daily cleaning into practice. Start with the small things; move on to the large.

Be aware that there may be a gap between a reaction you have, your perception of it, and the action to clean it. For my bookstore incident, my ability to locate and clean my negative perceptions quickly was an acquired skill. Prior to this breakthrough, it would often take days or weeks before I noticed that my energy was low and that I was judging myself or feeling victimized about an event.

As you pay attention to your energy levels, you will learn about your own patterns. This will give you the information you need for cleaning. For example, I noticed a pattern of major "dirt" arising inside me a couple of days after I made an important decision. I had registered for a very exciting workshop that was also very expensive. I knew it would change my life. For two days, I was joyous and had no doubt that I was making the right decision. On the third day, my energy plummeted. I was depressed, doubtful, and cynical. I knew that I had made the wrong decision. "What was I thinking? I cannot do this workshop at this time in my life! I do not have enough money, or time, or energy. What if I cannot pay my rent next month? What if I do not like the workshop?" I allowed my dire thoughts to pull me off center.

In the middle of my despair, I realized, "Maybe these thoughts are not real, but a backlash of fear." I made a note to pay attention the next time I made a positive, big decision in my life. And sure enough, three days after my next big life change, I went into fear and doubt. But this time I was conscious of the cycle. Because I was now aware of the pattern, I was able to accept these emotions for what they were: dirt. So I took a long, soapy bath, and imagined all my old fears and disaster thoughts going down the drain with my dirty bath water. Soon I was excited about my life and my choices again.

Cleaning allows for authentic centering. The practices at the end of this chapter will help you learn about your patterns and improve your short-term cleaning abilities.

They will guide you to hold more energy and gather the stamina for your long-term cleaning projects.

Long-Term Cleaning

The core agreements you made as a child will take a while to dissolve, because they are a part of a much greater societal structure. From what I've seen, these types of core agreements are at epidemic levels, and almost everyone is sick with false beliefs about self-worth. You do not need to judge yourself or feel guilty that you have core agreements, such as needing love and approval, feeling at your core that you are bad, or fearing that you are going to be abandoned. You are not flawed because you have these types of agreements! They are simply the root of what needs to be cleaned to live from your center. To address them, you'll want to roll up your sleeves and get ready to dig deep.

Long-term cleaning projects, such as the core belief "I need to be perfect to be okay," are best saved until you have the energy and time to dedicate yourself to them. By constantly perceiving and clearing out what attaches to your structure in the short-term, it is easier to track and monitor the deeper core agreements.

Long-term means long-term. Put things into perspective by counting up how many years you have been acting from a core belief in your life. If you have lived your life believing that you are not lovable or that you are undeserving, it will take some time to clean out all the manifestations of these beliefs. Don't be surprised when these issues keep appearing in your life, even long after you think you are done with them!

One thing I have discovered about our emotional closets is that they have trapdoors. Just when you think you have cleaned out a particular issue or structure, it seems to pop up again in a slightly different form. This points to a long-term cleaning issue. When you make space in your closet, the deeper issues then have room to emerge into the light.

When you are in disaster mind and a trapdoor opens with more stuff, you say, "Not again! I just cleaned that. I must be doing this wrong." When you come from clear mind, you are interested in this new appearance, whatever it is, and know that you are discovering a vast, hidden chamber within. Cleaning becomes exciting, because you know you are gathering the strength and vision to act on the old, musty foundational pieces that keep you out of balance. By not letting the debris of current events pile up, and by keeping track of the long-term projects, you will gather the energy to reclaim your natural joy.

Here's a great example of a long-term cleaning project. As Melanie started on a Toltec path of transformation and began to increase her awareness, she realized that she was terrified of disappointing people. Melanie always thought that her desire to be nice was a natural trait that allowed her to get along well with all types of people. But as she began to clean her old agreements, she saw that her being "nice" all the time was actually a fearful way to stay in control so that others wouldn't get upset with her.

When Melanie first realized her niceness was a cover-up for her fear, she dedicated herself to cleaning all the places in which she didn't speak her truth for fear of people's reactions. "I realized I avoided conflict by always trying to say what I thought the other person wanted to hear. I had done this for so long I didn't know what was true for me anymore." This was definitely a long-term cleaning project.

So that she wouldn't get overwhelmed, Melanie started small and picked one relationship from which to start clearing her old agreements and patterns: a coworker who was often frustrated with her. Each day she would pay attention to whether she was being nice as a deflection or from a genuine place.

"I found a whole host of agreements to clean as I watched myself with my coworker," Melanie said. "There were agreements that I wasn't good enough, that other people always knew better than me, that others' opinions were more valuable than mine, that if I shared my truth I would get in trouble."

Through her increased awareness and by journaling about each different agreement, Melanie was able to start separating out the different strands from the tangle of her stories. She could then clean them one at a time. Two of the main long-term cleaning tools she used were recapitulation (see the practices section), a Toltec technique of reclaiming energy from the past, and learning to consistently be open and breath through her fear of getting into trouble. As she used these tools repeatedly, over time her desire to be authentic overcame her old fears of disappointing others.

One thing to watch for during long-term cleaning: When you are not aware, you might believe that most of your problems stem from outside yourself. To make yourself feel better quickly, you may try to change and control the external. You might search for short-term cleaning solutions by focusing on the actions of the people around you: "If only my boss would not yell at me." "If only my wife would listen to me." "If only the world wasn't such a messed-up place." But by opening the closet door wide, you will discover that pretty much anything that *appears* external is actually an *internal* need for cleaning.

When you take honest responsibility for your emotional reactions and opinions, you see that your responses about others needing to change are cover-ups for where you either need to change or move on. Your emotional reactions to current events often have nothing at all to do with the present moment but are governed by what still needs to be cleaned from the past.

Do not fall into the trap of using your actions to clean up other people's stuff. Such efforts may seem a lot easier in the short-term, but they help no one in the long-term. This may be your first area of long-term cleaning—pulling your energy back to your own house! Right use of action is about taking responsibility for what is yours to clean. It can be easy to notice that your partner or your boss or your parents have full closets and dust bunnies under their sofas. If they invite you to share what you see, do so with utmost love and respect. Then create the space and encouragement for them to do their own cleaning.

To support long-term and short-term cleaning takes a conscious shift in attitude, and doing your internal cleaning not as a chore but as a prayer, brings a sense of sacredness into all your cleaning.

Cleaning as Art, Cleaning as Prayer

You can bring discouragement and annoyance to your cleaning projects, or you can bring love and joy. Notice how you clean your physical house. Is this a reflection of the energy that you bring to your internal cleaning? When dirty dishes pile up, do you put on music and dance while you do them, or do you wash them grudg-ingly, wishing they would go away? Do you take the time in your life to keep things neat, or do you rush around, always a little behind?

Sometimes cleaning is about letting the debris settle. If you go in with a blowtorch, determined to clear out everything right now, you will create more chaos than cleaning. If you have been triggered by something and are emotionally stirred up, allowing the dust to settle and the emotions to simmer down enables you to see clearly where to best put your energy. Patience will guide you to right use of action.

Cleaning of all forms can be a prayer. Each time I wash my dishes or scrub the floors, I honor the power of cleaning and am grateful for all the gifts in my life. Every time I place soap on my hands, I link it to the cleaning I am doing in my mind. Even when physical cleaning feels overwhelming, I start at one spot of a room and bless each object I touch. Instead of looking at the whole, I focus on the one area of this moment and keep working until it is completed—all in gratitude.

Your structures, whether you like them or not, have served you in some way. You built your energetic struc-tures to help you comprehend and manage your world. While you clean your old agreements and beliefs, thank them for all the ways that they have served you, then dismantle them piece by piece. Wash off the dirt of your judgments and release the need for things to be other than they are. To avoid being overwhelmed by the enor-mity of your task, keep your focus on one area, clear as much as you can, then move on. Gratitude and perseverance are the best form of elbow grease there is. Explore the beauty of what you are cleaning, and its perfection, as you release it.

As you clear and clean, treat yourself like a favorite child who, after a long day of play, returns home covered in mud and hair full of snarls and stickers. With all of your compassion, patience, and gentle care, sit yourself down and begin to wash off the mud and comb out the tangles.

Beneath the dirt and ratty hair lies a precious child, ready to love, open, and explore life.

Practices

Daily Cleaning: Recapitulation

One of the most powerful Toltec cleansing techniques is recapitulation. Recapitulation is a simple technique based on breathing and the use of a focused will to reclaim energy. Its purpose is to gather the energy that you lost during past interactions. Each day as you interact with the world, you lose some of your own energy and take on the thoughts, beliefs, and energy of others. Your disaster mind creates leaks in your vital energy, and your structure magnetizes familiar dirt. Recapitulation is a process of deliberate internal cleaning and untangling on an energetic level.

Recapitulation is a form of conscious cleaning that frees you from the energetic filaments that connect you to past events of your life. These energetic ties take you out of the moment, because whenever you experience similar circumstances, these threads are activated, pulling you into the past. Recapitulation reclaims this energy and releases the links to past events.

Reclaiming energy allows you to make dramatic changes in the present. There are different theories about how to do recapitulation. Toltec author Taisha Abelar spent the better part of a year visiting a cave each day and recapitulating her entire life. Victor Sanchez, a Toltec teacher and author, recommends building a box to use for doing all recapitulation work. I used to crawl under my desk to do my recapitulation practice, though now I often do it lying on my bed before I go to sleep or early in the morning. There are many Toltec books that explain the various recapitulation methods; see the bibliography at the end of this book for other resources.

There are three important parameters for doing a recapitulation: establishing a safe, comfortable, nondistracting space; setting your intent or will to reclaim your energy; and using your breath to pull in and reclaim energy. I like to imagine that the energy I am going to reclaim is pieces of light threads, and I use this visualization to breathe these filaments back into my body.

Whenever you do recapitulation, it is important to come from a place of love and acceptance. What you do not want to do is go back in your memory to a painful time and create more self-wounding by reliving all the emotions or by judging yourself or others involved or by reanalyzing the situation. Your purpose is simply to go back as a witness, with love and forgiveness, and reunite your energy to the present. If you feel emotions or judgment, then you are not ready to clean that particular event. Remember your periods and grammar; do not judge yourself for judging or comparing yourself.

My dear friend Larry Andrews introduced me to the idea of doing a short, daily recapitulation in the evenings before bed. I call this the five-minute quickie recapitulation technique. It is brief but very effective on many levels. This recapitulation method teaches you how to review your day and how to gather and clean yourself energetically by using the following steps.

1. Set your intent on why you want to create more energy in your life. Your intent can be broad: "I want extra energy to help me break down my old structures." Or your intent can be specific: "My intent is to recapitulate my energy so that I can release my jealousy of Marsha." Decide what you want to recapitulate in this session: Do you want to recapitulate a certain event or age, or are you simply going back to see where you lost energy today? Make this clear so that you can stay focused.

2. Connect your will to a higher energy source—the sun or earth work well. Do this by imagining a cord between your solar plexus and the sun or earth. You can also link to the four elements. This link will strengthen your practice.

3. Either sitting or lying comfortably, let your mind go back to the beginning of your day. See the circumstances, people, and places of your day as clearly as possible, without getting attached to the emotional aspects of each scene. Breathe back your energy from this scene by either visualizing your energy returning to you or feeling the energy coming into your body—or both. Make your breath audible. One great technique is to imagine yourself as a vacuum cleaner, inhaling your energy out of the scene.

   Pay attention into what part of your body you feel the energy coming back. Do not get caught in analyzing. Simply breathe in your energy. You can analyze and ponder later.

4. Breathe out any energy you took from someone else or any agreements you made at the time. (Remember, all this work is done with love, so if you begin to feel judgmental or angry, shift to recapitulating something that is not as painful emotionally.) Imagine breathing in your energy and breathing back any energy you may have taken on that does not belong to you. If you feel that you sent out some negative energy in the past, you can practice breathing this in and then breathing it down to the earth beneath you and letting the earth transform this old energy.

5. You may find your mind jumping from image to image. Keep breathing in your energy, and let be

whatever pictures might come up. You may need to bring yourself back to the scene you initially set out to recapitulate if you find that your mind is trying to drag you away from it.

6. Recapitulation can last for a brief time or for as long as you can stay focused. Keep remembering to return your awareness to your breath and your intent. The audible breath will help you stay focused. You can start from the beginning of your day and move to the present, start at the present and go backward through time to the beginning of your day, or let your mind reveal the places where you lost the most energy during the day. If other events or circumstances present themselves as you recapitulate, feel free to either ignore them or recapitulate them.

7. When you feel complete, take three deep breaths, and visualize that you are using light to clear out anything that does not belong to you in this moment. Release your connection to the earth, sun, or the four elements. You may want to say a prayer of thanks.

Over time, as you continue this practice, you will feel an increase of energy in your body.

You can also do mini-recapitulation sessions anytime during the day. Set your intent, call in the four elements, and consciously breathe back your energy.

Each day, you can find a few minutes to spare, so any protests that "I do not have time for this" are not true.

Spend the next week giving yourself at least five minutes every evening to recapitulate your day. When you recapitulate daily, you will soon see how you gain energy to use for bigger cleaning projects. You will also strengthen your tracking skills.

People doing daily recapitulation often notice that their dreams change. This is a sign of increased personal energy. Instead of spending your dreamtime processing your day, you clear your dreaming palate to taste other forms of dreaming.

Recapitulation can be done for ten to fifteen minutes or longer. When I worked with don Miguel, our community gathered together once a week for extended sessions of recapitulation. Working with a group is a powerful way to increase the energy and go deeper. If you have extra time and energy, you can always do an extended recapitulation. Picking a specific topic (my first relationship, my last job, my fear of spiders) guides and supports your work.

To support your practice, you may wish to use my audio CD, *Returning to Center: Meditations and Recapitulation,* which thoroughly describes the recapitulation process and leads you through a fifteen-minute guided recapitulation. See the resources section at the back of the book for more information.

The Art of Sorting

This exercise is a continuation of the mind exploration and tracking exercises discussed in the last chapter. You can use it in conjunction with recapitulation.

Continue to witness and take notes of your thoughts and experiences. Begin to sort them: What are your short-term cleaning projects? What are your long-term cleaning projects? Track your short-term projects to discern what the deeper structure might be.

If you have nonjudgmental, clear friends who know you well, ask them to help you see any hidden agreements that may not be noticeable to you because of the cleverness of your gremlins.

You do not need to remember how you created the structure, but by keeping your awareness high and watching your gremlins, you can begin to make educated guesses. For at least a month, keep a log of what you find, noting your perceptions and any information you get from friends. Then make very clear action steps for short-term cleaning. Have a second list of actions ready for when you have more energy to focus on long-term cleaning.

Keep your lists handy as valuable resources to refer to when dirt arises or when you feel ready to roll up your sleeves and scrub the deeper layers of dirt.

Connecting to the Element of Fire

Cleaning means letting go of the past and embracing the present moment. Here is a short practice for connecting the element of fire and the art of cleaning. It is especially potent after doing recapitulation.

Read through the gremlin tactics again. On five small pieces of paper, write down five ways you sabotage, distract, or limit yourself. Build a fire in your fireplace, make a bonfire outside, or put equal parts rubbing alcohol and Epsom salts into a fireproof container and light—this burns beautifully. Two layers of aluminum foil formed in a shallow bowl over an old pot works well for burning this mixture, or use a large metal container on bricks.

Hold your papers in your hand and close your eyes. Ask yourself if you are really ready to let go of these tactics. If you are, thank them out loud one by one. This honors that the gremlins' initial intent was to keep you safe and lets them know that you are now ready to live another way. For example: "Thank you for constantly projecting my fears that other people will not like me."

After you speak your word or sentence of thanks, say out loud, "I now release you to the fire of change," and put the paper into the fire. Feel the fire within consuming these old beliefs as you watch the fire turn the paper into ash.

Repeat this exercise as often as you like. By doing this practice, you will become adept at noticing what you want to release, thanking it, and then letting it go into the cleansing fire of your spirit.

Inner Guidance

Fire Visualization for Creating a New Container

Your second guardian is from the element of fire. From fire you learn the art of inner cleaning—the right use of action.

While either sitting or lying down, take some deep breaths into your belly. Imagine yourself standing in the middle of your beautiful stone circle. Face your symbol for the element of air and say hello. Now move a quarter turn to the right and ask for guidance and energy from the element of fire to give yourself the courage and strength to open the door of your inner closet.

Invite a fire guide to join you and support you in taking responsibility for cleaning your structure. Be open to how that guide may appear. Your fire guide may be an animal, a person you know, or a stranger. It may be a quiet voice in your head or a knowing in your body. Your guardian of fire may not come to you immediately, but later in a dream or while you are in the middle of your day, this guide may appear. Pray for the power to clean even the toughest dirt with grace and joy.

When you feel complete, ask for a symbol to represent this new anchor, and let this symbol hold the fire direction of your circle. Then imagine the circle dissolving. It is always helpful to write down what you perceived and any messages you received from fire.

To link your visualization back into your life, place an object on your altar to represent fire and your new intent: a candle, a washcloth, or any object that pleases you. Ask to use all of the elements and their gifts wisely to guide you through cleaning your old structure and coming to center in your authentic self.

5

Water:
The Art of Opening

Flowing with Infinite Possibility

When one door of happiness closes,
another opens; but often we look so long
at the closed door that we do not see the
one which has been opened for us.

—Helen Keller

As you continue your journey to clear your vision and clean your being, a third aspect needs to be addressed: your emotions. When you open and acknowledge your emotions, you allow cleansing waters to flow. Flowing water has huge power. It will dissolve what is stuck and unblock what is jammed within.

The gift of water is the art of opening. Not just opening to the things or experiences you like but learning to open to *all* things. It is effortless to stay open to things you like or that feel good; it is much more difficult to stay open to things you dislike or that feel bad. To open means accepting all that life brings while simultaneously choosing to act for positive change. By staying equally open to the "good" and the "bad" feelings, you create space to allow healing to dissolve your old structure.

Opening is not a passive mood of discouraged acceptance toward your inner world or outer reality. It is a courageous internal movement of trust in the unfolding of life.

Many religions use water as a means to purify and open to spirit. Before entering the mosque to pray, Moslems respectfully wash their hands and feet. Christians are baptized to purify themselves and open themselves to accept God. Many shamanic traditions use water to create sacred space before a ceremony. When we align with the element of water, we connect with many practices of purification to prepare for something new.

Opening allows us to release assumptions, allows the opportunity for miracles to occur, and provides room for spirit to enter. It frees what is not longer useful and expands us beyond the known.

Dissolving What Is Stuck

A great story about the power of water comes from a master of yoga, Yogi Bhajan, and it was "Peggyized" and passed on to my by my mentor and friend Peggy Dylan. Imagine your unconscious as a dirty pan of oil. Whenever you do any healing work, it is like pouring pure, clear water into the pan of oil. What happens when water and oil come together? Since oil and water do not mix, the oil will start rising to the surface. The oil represents all of your old emotions and agreements. So as the water of clarity pours in, the difficult emotions come to the surface (and become conscious). Can you remain open to everything that arises so that it can overflow and be released?

Whenever you create more flow around your stagnant structure, long-forgotten emotions begin to float into your conscious mind. Your initial reaction may be to resist these old emotions. This resistance arises because, early on, you learned to shut down the uncomfortable parts of your conscious mind. You might think, "If I pretend my closet is already clean, maybe no one will notice," or "If I keep the door closed long enough, perhaps the gremlins and monsters will go away."

You may believe that if you close down your senses, if you keep all the taps of your emotions shut off, you will stay safe. But imagine living in a house where all the drains are clogged with old sludge, and you refuse to turn on the water for fear of what might overflow. Soon, not only do you have the backlog of sludge but also overflowing toilets and of piles of unwashed clothes.

This tactic of keeping your emotions dammed up may have once worked to some extent. When you were a child, it may have allowed you to survive in overwhelming emotional situations. But as an adult, closing down strengthens the rigid structures that limit you. The same responses that helped you survive the ups and downs of your childhood now keep you from being flexible and present as an adult.

For example, the thought "Mom loves my brother more than me" could become the belief that no one could ever really love you. Every time you are in a relationship and feel loved, that new energy would flow around your old "no one loves me" agreement. Getting the love you so desperately crave would be like pouring clear water into your being and stirring to the surface all the mud of old emotions. Your fear of abandonment and loss might arise. Without awareness, you might unconsciously create a drama to explain your emotions, then blame your partner for your uncomfortable feelings.

The pattern of closing becomes so habitual that it is hard to recognize. With practice you can learn to notice when you are closing, before you start making up stories and intensifying the emotions.

Here is a good way to begin to sense the difference in your being between staying open or closing. Shut your eyes and feel in your body a time you took something very personally, a time when you felt offended or angry or resentful of someone else's actions. It may be something that happened yesterday or something that happened ten years ago. Visualize something that was very painful at the time. How did your body feel? Take a moment to experience the emotions and sensations in your body while you remember something that hurt you.

Most of us feel a constriction, a tightening in our body, when we take something personally. There is a feeling of becoming smaller, of closing in. The mind perceives that we are being judged or wronged in some way, and our old thoughts trigger our emotional body.

Now feel a time when you could have taken something personally, but did not—perhaps something in the past that would normally have hurt you, but this particular time it did not. How did your body feel? How did this feel different from when you took something personally? Notice if any images or symbols arise to show the difference between these two states of being.

When you do not take an event or confrontation personally, there is a sense of fluidity in the body. You keep your happiness and balance because you are open. Instead of feeling the grip and weight of your structure, you feel the space of your true being.

When you open, you allow old emotions to flow through you on their way out, rather than stagnating. Resisting old emotions only keeps out authentic healing. A stream blocked by debris will become stagnant. Removing dead leaves and trash allows for cleansing flow. Open the faucets and let the plumbing in your house function as it is meant to.

Why Resistance Is Futile

Resisting, or wishing things were different, is a way you likely close around pain. Another way is to compare yourself to others. You cause most of your own suffering not because of the actual emotional pain, but because of your reaction to it.

As you release your need to control your emotions, you align with the natural flow of energy. When you do not resist your structure while simultaneously not believing in it, you reclaim strength from it.

Resistance stops the flow of energy. If the voice of the old structure is talking loudly, and your reaction is to try to fight it, the only thing that wins is the old structure, for it now has your undivided attention. Resistance is the opposite of opening. By staying aware, you can use your emotions as a way to uncover the underlying structure.

When I first starting working with don Miguel Ruiz and the Toltec community, my resistance was fierce. I prided myself on being tough and independent. The truth is, I was terrified of disapproval. I would often spend the first two days of a workshop struggling with enormous resistance to any new information. My structure was being threatened, and I felt as if I were fighting with all my might to keep from drowning.

One of my big shifts happened when I stopped judging my own resistance and opened beyond what I knew. This happened gradually, culminating in an experience in Peru in the late 1990s. My dear friend and mentor Gini was determined to support me in moving beyond my self-importance and need for approval. She hatched a plan with don Miguel and asked me to not teach or talk to anyone for the first five days of the trip; instead, I was to focus on being in service to everyone on the journey.

Shifting from being a teacher to being in silence was okay at first. I practiced paying attention to everything around me and being open. That lasted for about one day. Then my structure started to assert itself. By day two, I was starting to see that I had things I wanted to share. I was important. I had a right to teach. "Why is Gini doing this to me? She is obviously trying to control me." I bounced from self-criticism to severe judgment to terror to resistance to anger. I was not being valued! I was being ignored! I wanted to fight for my rights! I knew there was a lesson in there somewhere, but my own resistance stopped me from seeing what it was.

One morning, Gini asked me to help her plan a ceremony with the group. Planning a ceremony is one of my favorite things to do, but at this moment I exploded angrily, as if she had asked me to clean a hundred toilets. I think I cursed at Gini and ran out the door. I was furious. How dare she think she could make me be in silence for days on end, then ask me to create a ceremony! How dare she!

Looking back, my strong reaction now seems comical. But at the time, I was so pushed by my own need to be independent and important that I was blind. I knew that a spiritual person is not supposed to be in resistance, but there I was. I stormed out of the hotel and furiously walked into Machu Picchu. It was raining hard, but I decided to climb Waynu Picchu, a beautiful, sacred, and very steep mountain at the edge of the city.

My anger kept growing as I climbed the mountain. I could not decide if I should toss myself off the cliff for being such a miserable excuse of a spiritual being or go back and yell at Gini for mistreating me. The rain intensified, and the stone steps became steeper and more slippery. I soon came to a point of choice. I knew I could hold onto my anger, or I could continue up the mountain. I did not have the energy to do both. As I took the next step, I opened to releasing my anger. I surrendered. I stopped resisting my own resistance and watched the emotions and struggle wash away with the rain as I continued to climb.

What caused me to resist being in silence was what Gini calls "a perceived threat to your image." My image was telling me, "If you were really important and a good girl, you would be teaching instead of being quiet and serving. If you were really spiritual, you would be okay with being in service. If you were special, you would get the lesson."

My point of choice was simple: to remain closed or to open. By a gift of grace (and pure exhaustion), I chose to open and keep moving on my path and up the mountain. I saw there was nothing to defend or fight against. As I climbed Waynu Picchu, my heart opened. I simply was. I did not need to be right. Everything melted. I stopped identifying with my old stories and let go of my need to be seen in any particular way.

When you fight against your stories, they gain energy.

When I hear people say, "I am never, ever going to do that again!" it is fairly certain they will be doing just that in the near future. When you open and say, "Thank you, agreement, for the ways you have served me. I release you and choose to accept love," you take the power from the old structure and give it to the new.

When you open, you become so much larger than your fears; they are like spider webs instead of barbed wire. But when you fight your own structure, you cut yourself on its sharp edges. As you surrender to the immense flow between the solidity of your structure, you will soon tap into an ocean of new resources and options.

Opening beyond Fear

Fear traps you under the weight of your emotions. When you think the emotions will never end and you close down, you might feel that you are drowning and that there is no way out. You grasp for something to hang on to, and your panic increases.

As you open to the flow of your emotions, keep your eyes open. You will learn to swim with the current—not to fight it, but to stay aware as it flows through you. You will become an underwater explorer, a fish able to breathe water through your heart.

One day a student, who was in great fear at the time, called me on the phone. After years of numbness, Michael was starting to experience his emotions. As a child, he had witnessed his father, who was an alcoholic, beat his mother. To cope, he had closed the door on his emotions. Now as he was opening the door to healing, the intensity of his repressed fear and anger at his father scared him, and he was starting to shut down again in an effort to make the pain stop. He imagined all of his emotions spilling out of an overflowing box and drowning him. Michael's impulse was to slam the lid down and stop the flow.

I said to him, "Instead of using the fear as a trigger to shut down, can you keep a tiny crack open for love to enter? Your fear is a sign of transformation, not a warning to stop." Later, he told me that he had imagined putting the lid on his box loosely and invited healing to enter into his pain. He still felt his emotions, but his awareness had expanded to hold the box and its contents in his hands. Michael found spaciousness for clearing his repressed emotions and saw that after years of numbness, the fear was actually telling him that he was on the right track.

Your energetic structure is a living being. It is held together by your belief in it, and it is fed by your energy. You created it to help yourself feel safe and to make sense of the world around you. As you journey deeper into yourself, you start to weaken the old structure. Emotions get shaken up. And of course your body becomes fearful. Your disaster mind starts yelling, "Danger! Danger!" and triggers your emotions to bounce all over the place. This is normal.

When you hit tremendous fear within yourself, this is sometimes a signal that you are moving through the shaky floor of your past agreements and toward the authentic foundation within. How wonderful! Do not use this fear to dissuade you from your task. Fear is energy. Move fear into excitement by accepting the fear and allowing it to flow into something new. Instead of saying to yourself, "I am afraid, I am afraid, I can't do this," start saying, "I am excited. I am willing to be uncomfortable. I am excited about transforming my fears into love by not judging myself."

Don Miguel taught me a wonderful lesson about jumping into the waters of your fear over and over again as a way of healing. In 1996, don Miguel came close to drowning during a journey to Palenque, Mexico. Two years later, I went snorkeling with him in Maui. We put a life vest on him, and he eagerly jumped into the water, only to madly scramble out again. As he sat panting on the deck of the boat, I asked him what was wrong.

"This is the first time I have been in the water since I almost drowned," he said, "and my body remembers the fear. Okay!" he said, and smiling at me, he jumped back into the water.

I watched him jump in and get out of the water three or four times, each time with less panic. Soon he was paddling around in the water happily. Don Miguel modeled how to open to fear and move beyond it by being willing to smile, then with awareness plunge in again and again until the fear diminished. He did not close down and say, "I should not feel this fear," or "The fear means I should not get in the water." His intent was to enjoy the water, and so he simply kept showing his body it was safe until it trusted again.

At the pivotal times in your life, remember the larger perspective of what you are doing. If you pay attention only to the fear, you will back off, and nothing will change. If you open to bigger sight, you will see the perfection of your terror, the rightness of being uncomfortable. You are actively dismantling the old and making room for the new. Keep jumping in with your heart open until the fear subsides.

Staying Open

There are times when you will see an old agreement or a pattern of thinking, know how it is hurting you, and choose to continue your behavior. If you do this, do not judge yourself; stay open to the ramifications of that agreement in your life. Sometimes it is too scary to release the old behavior, or you still have something to learn from it. Stay open. Sometimes you do not quite have the energy to make the change. Be gentle with yourself. Keep your awareness and your heart open, and you will gradually take yourself into a new way of being.

Sometimes, our greatest awakenings happen in the most difficult situations. What is revealed during these times can be shocking. One of the best times to practice opening is when you are overwhelmed. Can you open to whatever is in the present moment? "Oh, now I feel terror in my body. I open to this terror and let it move through me." "Ah, I feel closed and numb and unavailable. It is okay to be closed."

I was in a romantic relationship a while ago that was very painful. We seemed to bring out the worst in each other. I was miserable, trying to figure out "What part of this dynamic is mine, what is his, and why is it so hellish?" Despite much love between us, the drama was intense. One week we battled yet again, and I prayed that I would do something different this time. I decided to go fully into the emotions that were coming up, to open to them. I let go of the thoughts I was holding on to, such as, "He is making me feel this way," or "I am bad for feeling this way," and slid into the current of emotion.

The emotions were as intense as before I let go, but I maintained my open awareness. I felt my pain very deeply as part of me stayed open and curious. When I came out the other side, I felt that something I could not name had been cleaned and purified within me. I was better able to listen openly to my partner without judgment or fear.

Soon after this experience, I heard myself thinking, "I just want to be loved!" I stopped and opened to this thought: "I just want to be loved. I just want to be loved." Then I saw that if my full being was aligned with being loved, I feel loved.

I asked myself, "If you look openly at what you have created in this relationship, what do you really want?"

And the answer I heard was: "To be punished because I am bad."

Now that was not the answer I was expecting. I almost dismissed it as some random thought. But since I had so recently witnessed myself go through intense emotional upheaval, I paid attention. At that point, it was not important for me to figure out where I took on an agreement as strange as "I need to be punished." The source was not important, but what I was doing with it was. Did I really want to be punished? Was that my deepest truth?

The truth was I usually felt a low level of guilt and therefore needed to be punished. When I looked at my relationship, I realized that this was clearly being reflected back to me. If I'd wanted to be loved unconditionally, I would have been loved unconditionally. But since I wanted to be punished, I was getting emotionally beaten up. It was a perfect setup. I was getting exactly what some part of me was asking for. Strange but true.

As I opened to clarity, the muck of my old agreements arose into my conscious mind, and I could then make a conscious choice. When I saw this agreement, I did not make it anybody's fault. I did not spend a lot of time trying to figure out where it came from. Instead I just said to myself, "I don't want that anymore. I'm done. I am ready to release it." Eventually this caused it to dissolve, since I had opened to no longer believing the old agreement. The clear water of opening to acknowledge this agreement allowed the oil it had created to float up and out.

From the Divine to the Screaming Child

The gift of opening to change in your life allows you to move smoothly through transitions from an old structure to a new one, while maintaining your center. You are willing to see what you are doing and to take responsibility for your actions, no matter what they are. You learn to accept and love all aspects of yourself, from the divine to the screaming child. Each emotion, and each reaction, teaches you something new; it offers you another pearl when you keep your eyes and heart open.

Here are some tips to facilitate your process of opening.

Patience: Opening is a gradual process. Be patient with yourself. You do not wake up one day and say, "Hey, I think I'll open to this immense pain I am in." It takes practice and persistence. The truth is that each of us knows how to open. We do this naturally when we feel safe. We can also learn to open when we do not feel safe or when we feel challenged in some way.

Find the Source: As you increase your openness, you begin to see that most of your emotional reactions are not about the present at all. Keep opening the doors into the past, and you will often track the real source of your pain. Seek out the scared child, the lonely teenager. What agreements might they have made?

Embracing: When you find a frightened and confused part of yourself, embrace it with open arms. Intimacy is showing up for yourself, whether you are feeling on top of the world or terrified. Make space for all of your emotional self.

Healing: Sometimes you search for and find agreements that are causing your suffering. Other times you do not need to search but only to make space for the shift to occur. Opening itself is all that is needed to release the old. Your disaster mind might be yelling and screaming the entire time, your body may be in fear, and the healing will still occur. Stay open to the possibility of being a tiny bit more open than before.

Releasing: Any preconceived ideas of whom you believe you should be in the world or what your role is can cause you to close when the world around you changes. If you notice yourself feeling lost or disheveled when change occurs, open to explore if it is time to release whom you thought you were or where you thought you should be in favor of lovingly being with what is now.

Daily Practice: Like clear perception and active cleaning, opening is best practiced daily. What is important is not the amount you open but the consistent thread of teaching yourself to open as an automatic response. It is the effort, not the immediate results, that matters.

Gratitude: When you go into gratitude, you open. When you think of someone you love, you open. When you see a baby or a puppy, you open. Study this sensation in your body. What does it feel like when you open? What causes you to open? What causes you to close down?

Stretching: In this moment, what can you do to open just a little bit more? Try shifting your posture or taking a deep breath or thinking of a specific color filling your body. Does a particular movement or color or thought help you to open? Each moment, notice and play with what will open you just a tiny bit more. Focus only on the present moment. You will notice that an easy way to close down is to think of the future or to compare yourself to someone else. Your journey to opening lies in this moment. Be where you are and, with compassion, gently open in this moment.

Allowing Pure Emotions

Progress does not mean not having emotions. Being centered is accepting and opening to whatever emotions are present. Deeper and deeper levels will continue to emerge. As the trapdoors open wide and unconscious agreements surface, more cleaning occurs. Be aware that the deeper you go, the more intense the feelings may become. This is not a failure but a blessing. The question is: Are you willing to release and open to something greater? Can you find excitement even in the discomfort of your familiar structure dissolving?

As your emotional body heals, you may begin to experience pure emotions, separate from any story or belief. After the end of one relationship, I spent a year watching my guilt. I started by noticing when I felt guilty and tracking it to an immediate source. Then I started tracking it back to a possible past source. In the end, I realized that I had always felt guilty. Period. There was no way I was acting to create guilt in my life or anything looming from my past to account for it. I could invent all sorts of stories to find a way for the guilt to make sense, but they were simply that—stories.

The truth is, we live in a very guilt-ridden culture. I absorbed it. Period. Recognizing that it was not mine, I could open to it and let it go. When it arose, I could say, "Oh, look, it is guilt," and open to releasing it. If I had continued to clamp down on the guilt, what do you think would have happened?

To help you foster your new relationship with your emotional body, be mindful of the ways your mind tries to control or trigger your emotional body with its stories and fears. So often, when you shine the light of clarity on your thoughts and open to your emotions without story, they dissolve or easily flow through your being, leaving behind more spaciousness and joy. When you open and release your old emotions by being willing to simply witness them, your emotional body is able to function as it is supposed to. Then new emotions do not stick, but move through quickly and cleanly. A healed emotional body connects you to your intuition and to sensing guidance and information that is beyond the mind.

As you continue to open, self-discovery and learning become a joy. You move from resistance and fear to pouring more water into your being, becoming openly curious about what will come up next. Fear and the many emotions that stem from fear—such as anger, justification, and resistance—will arise and fall.

And the reverse is also true; happiness, love, and acceptance will also arise and fall. Don't attach to any one state. Like the flow of water, none of these emotions are permanent. Allow them to move naturally through you, and hold your still center point within. You are not your emotions, just as you are not your thoughts. Embrace them both as your children, love and support them in maturing, but don't let them run your household!

In the next chapter, you will learn how to further support a healthy emotional body by learning a new way to be in relationship with your physical body.

Practices

Investigating Closing

Write down six things that cause you to close or put up a wall to block out a feeling or a person. For example:

my boss when she gets angry

the thought of war

when I feel jealous

when the company sends a memo that they are having more job cuts

when I take responsibility for other people's emotions

when I'm not sure if I can pay all the bills

Take a couple of minutes to examine each of these six things, then write down exactly what it is that causes you to close: What is the core, the foundational image or emotion, that makes you close down?

Emotionally, keep investigating why you would need to close down, say, when you can't pay your bills or when your boss gets angry at you. It is not the bills themselves or your boss's anger that causes you to close, but the thought about what those things mean. Your mind might say, "But of course I close when my boss is angry; I have to protect myself." Or "Of course I close when I am afraid I can't pay my bills: that is real." It is real when you have a need to feel safe or are in fear, but the question is: Does your closure help you grow or pay the bills? Fear and worry try to pretend they are your friends, but they only create tension, stress, and unease.

Pick one of these reactions and practice opening to it a little bit each day. Tell yourself the truth: My boss is angry. Period. I am afraid I can't pay my bills. Period. Then carefully watch the thoughts and emotions that arise as you practice opening to these statements. These thoughts will show you the structure that keeps you closed. Clean out what is not yours by doing recapitulation or by imagining a sparkling stream running through your emotional body until it clears all the clogged and muddy channels. Once you have created more space, open to more possibilities and creative solutions.

The beauty of opening to difficult thoughts or emotions is that we allow more resources and inspirations to flow and release the stories that cause us to suffer.

Opening to New Possibilities

Often we close down because our disaster mind is telling us a story based on past events; we believe the story, and it triggers an old emotional response. Each time you notice disaster mind telling you a story that causes you to close, or you feel your emotional body going into an old fear, make up at least three different stories that help you open. The more outrageous the story is, the better.

Making up new stories changes the emotions in your body and will sometimes completely shift the dynamic. In any case, a new story will shift your response to the disaster mind/emotional reaction pattern, which is the most important thing.

Sometimes the stories will come in hindsight. Write them down. Eventually, you will be able to make up stories in the present moment. This is a great way to break up your rigid thinking and structures and create more space. The more humor you can bring to this process, the better.

Here is an example from our list above.

"I close when the company sends a memo that they are doing more job cuts."

Notice what the disaster story is and what happens in your emotional body.

"Larry got laid off last year and still hasn't found a job. If I lose my job I'll never find another one . . ."

Now consciously shift your story:

"Getting laid off could be the best thing that ever happens to me. I've wanted to do something new, and this might be the perfect opportunity. I might not get laid off because, as the company explores what it needs, it will discover how valuable I am. Maybe I'll even get a raise and a reward party for how fabulous I am!"

So what if this new story is not true? The emotions stirred up by your disaster mind are not based in reality either! Use this Toltec technique of creating a new story to have some fun and get out of a stuck pattern at the same time.

Keep shifting the story until you get some relief in your emotional body, and you start opening to new possibilities rather than cycling the same story and traumatizing your emotional body about some imagined future.

Connecting to the Element of Water

When you are focusing on staying open and letting old emotions come to the surface, it is really helpful to get your physical body into water. Immersing yourself in a river or lake or your bathtub will calm your emotional body, and it reminds me of the nature of fluidity. Do not hesitate to use the element of water extensively as you work with your emotional body.

To connect to the element of water, consciously prepare a bath for yourself. Use Epsom salts and essential oils. As you soak in the bath, imagine the water seeping into you and dissolving your old structure or any stuck emotions. Let yourself be held by the water, and allow the water to open you. Accept all of your emotions, let them flow, then invite the water to wash them away. When you feel complete, pull the plug and visualize letting everything go down the drain.

You can do a mini-version of this practice by consciously connecting to water every time you wash your hands and reminding yourself about the power of accepting the flow of life. Experiences, like emotions, come and go in the cycle of life.

Inner Guidance

Water Visualization for Creating a New Container

Your third guardian is the element of water. From water you learn the art of opening—the right use of your emotional flow.

Let your body be comfortable, and take some deep breaths into your belly. Imagine yourself standing in the middle of your beautiful stone circle. Greet your symbols for the elements of air and fire. Make a quarter turn to the right of fire, and ask for guidance and energy from the element of water to give you the willingness and faith to surrender to what is.

Invite a water guide to join you and support you in releasing your resistance and contraction. Be open to how that guide may appear. Your water guide may be an animal, a person you know, or a stranger. It may be a quiet voice in your head or a knowing in your body. Your guardian of water may not come to you immediately, but later in a dream or while you are in the middle of your day, water may show its many forms to you. Pray for the grace to open and expand in difficult times.

When you feel complete, ask for a symbol to represent this new anchor, and place it in the water direction of your circle.

For your altar, pick an object to represent water and place it in one of the directions on the outside of the circle. You can represent water with a bowl of water, a statue of a dolphin, or any object that pleases you. Set your intent to use all of the elements and their gifts to guide you through the places where you close down, riding the flow of your emotions to your center.

6

Earth:
The Art of Nourishing

Feeding Your Depths

We must learn not to disassociate the
airy flower from the earthy root, for
the flower that is cut off from its root
fades, and its seeds are barren; whereas
the root, secure in Mother Earth, can
produce flower after flower and bring
their fruit to maturity.

—Kabbalah

The final element in your circle is earth. Earth represents your physical body and the need to nourish yourself from the inside out. Opening allows us to delve into and clean the darker aspects of our being; the earth's nourishing aspects feed your center so that you can become more deeply grounded in self-love and self-respect.

The foundations of your life are based on the false beliefs you made as a child or agreements that were passed down to you. As the structure built on this faulty base begins to crack apart, the temptation is to buttress it and reinforce it with duct tape. If you let the old foundation fall apart, you may feel that there will be nothing to hold you steady. But underneath this false foundation is the true solidity of your being.

The fourth element teaches you to send your roots into your true soil.

My favorite analogy for this concept comes from farming. Conventional farming focuses on keeping pests and diseases away from crops, using pesticides and herbicides. The results are toxic plants and soil that is slowly poisoned. Fertilizers are then used on the depleted soil to give the plants what they need to grow.

Organic farming focuses on keeping the soil and crops healthy. Organic farmers know that strong, healthy plants resist pests and diseases. The result is an emphasis on feeding the soil. Since each plant has different nutritional requirements, the soil is constantly tested and supplemented.

If you treat yourself the way conventional farmers treat their crops, you act to defend yourself from outside invaders. You use judgment, criticism, and comparison as your weapons. In the process, your own soil becomes toxic. You falsely believe you nourish yourself by keeping out what you do not like. But the truth is that you are only poisoning yourself.

If you treat yourself the way organic farmers treat their crops, you keep your attention within and focus on your own soil. You constantly ask, "What do I need to nourish myself in this moment?" Instead of fighting or trying to change the outside world, you strengthen the inner foundation.

Nourishing Your Own Soil

How do you learn to nourish your own soil when so many weedlike thoughts and fears are clamoring for attention? How do you get beneath the shell of your false foundation, which demands the toxicity of judgment to hold it together? What really nourishes your base?

Nourishment is the culmination of the earlier gifts of air, fire, and water. With air's clear perception, you learn to see your true needs rather than your surface structure. Fire's cleaning uncovers the neglected places and makes space for new agreements. Water's opening increases your self-intimacy and informs you of where you need nourishing.

After cleaning and opening, nourishment is what you put into the space you have created. Nourishing is an art, a response to your deepest longing. Beneath the voices of the mind and your fearful emotions, a whisper of authentic need echoes. The structure yells to you, "I need to feel safe. I need to be protected. I need your attention." The shaky foundation beneath it claims that it must be bolstered to keep everything in your life safe.

Your authentic foundation—your root system—whispers, "Look deeper. You are safe. The love is within." True nourishment helps you to support and strengthen this presence.

Nourishing yourself includes a willingness to discover what feeds your authenticity. You learn to nourish your roots by using your outer and inner life to guide you. The result is a new structure, rooted in love and acceptance. From this sacred soil, you can truly extend your roots and grow.

Like your other new tools of perception, cleaning, and opening, nourishing takes practice and experimentation. There are seeds of love and seeds of fear within you. What you nourish will grow. To flourish, your being requires unconditional and consistent care. The soil of your inner self needs to be watered and fed. Sporadic attention, flooding then drought, or giving too many of your nutrients to others all weaken your core and stunt your development.

True nourishment comes drop by drop. Choosing to shift your perception is an act of nourishment. Cleaning out a reaction based on fear is an act of nourishment. Opening just that little bit more is an act of nourishment.

Cravings and Needs of the Body

Care is needed to discern the blurry boundary between nourishing your true self and nourishing your false structure. Sometimes, what feels truly nourishing in the moment is toxic in the long run, and what feels uncomfortable or even frightening in the short term is deeply nourishing in the long term.

When you begin to conceptualize your life as a process of long-term nourishment instead of short-term pleasure, the choices are easier.

An easy way to see this dynamic is with food. Many foods feel great in the short run, but in the long run can be very destructive. You may crave toxic foods, such as sugar and caffeine, even if they are hurting you. Only when you go beneath their addictive nature do you feel what your body really wants: healthy, sustaining food.

The same thing is true for toxic thoughts and actions. Conscious awareness teaches you what your true cravings are. When you are unconscious, you act in the short term, for the immediate fix. As you nourish your awareness, you will begin to see the ramifications of your actions. You will gain valuable information when you listen to the body as a guide and watch what you create in your life, always with an eye toward long-term, sustainable nourishment.

As part of this process, when you eat any type of "food,"—whether it is physical, emotional, or mental— you learn to ask yourself, "What is this nourishing?" "Is this food creating fear or joy?" "Is this toxic or sustaining?"

Simple witnessing teaches you what you are nourishing and gives you the opportunity to shift. Remember, you may witness the toxic effects of a behavior for a while before you have the energy to shift it. Be patient and allow yourself the space without judgment to make the change.

Openly listen to your impulses. Do they take you toward acceptance and joy or toward fear and contraction? As you explore, you will learn to distinguish the impulses of long-term nourishment versus short-term relief.

Imagine yourself as a plant ready to flower. Start by honoring your roots. For humans, the roots are your simple bodily needs: good sleep, good food, exercise, loving touch. Make sure you start here. Pay attention to how much sleep your body needs. Take note of how different foods shift your moods and sense of physical well-being. Getting clear on these basics will solidify your new foundation.

How you care for your body affects your emotions, energy, and perception. You may notice many things that you want to change about your basic habits. Do not try to make too many changes at once. Pick a few to focus on, create the change, and move on to the next. Do not sabotage yourself by taking on so much that you become overwhelmed. Nourishing is a gradual, moment-by-moment process. Like cleansing, nourishing is not something that is done just once.

During a Crisis

Remembering how to nourish yourself in the middle of an emotional crisis is tricky. When you feel good, it is easier to recognize what is sustaining and what is toxic. But when you get caught in an old emotion, when you feel scared or out of control or insecure, you revert back to toxic thoughts and behaviors. You judge and compare yourself. Or you see yourself as a helpless victim without any power. Or you stop taking responsibility for yourself. You plunge into disaster mind and project your fears onto others. These behaviors encourage your old structure but starve your inner being.

It takes great awareness to see your behaviors and even greater courage and energy to change them. This change comes from learning to nourish yourself in spite of, and through, your fear and judgment. Compassion, patience, humor, and trust are needed. When you feel that you are falling on your face, expressing these qualities to yourself is difficult but crucial. Nourish yourself through all phases of the healing cycle.

I recently heard a great story about choosing to nourish oneself despite an embarrassing situation. One day, my friend Maria filled her diesel truck with unleaded gasoline. "Usually, I would have judged myself horribly. Instead, I noticed my mistake, called a friend to come help me out, and waited. My mind stayed clear, and I spent the time stretching and breathing, helping myself get more present. It was exciting to make a mistake and realize I could still be good to myself!"

Just the way water soaks into the earth, our intent to nurture ourselves soaks into our being. Our minds may tell us, "Nothing is growing; nothing is changing; this is hopeless," but our bodies are soaking in new nutrients. Eventually the seeds of love will manifest in our lives. Each tiny act of compassion or forgiveness or joy, even if we do not feel it in the moment, soaks through the framework of our structure and activates our new foundation.

Breaking Habitual Patterns

The process works best when you remain aware and continually clear out what no longer sustains you. Something that nourished you in the past may one day be toxic. Something that appears toxic may be vitally nourishing. Be willing to investigate, to ask questions, to watch, and to wait.

Here are two stories about breaking habitual patterns and learning new ways to nourish your body. The first story explores the pathway to releasing serious addictions, and the other is about how to release a habit that was once nourishing but became toxic.

Sally had struggled most of her adult life with an addiction to alcohol. When she felt alone or scared, she would stay up all night drinking vodka. Hardly anyone knew about her struggles with alcohol, and whenever she committed to herself that she would stop drinking, she would go on another binge. When I first met her, she shared her shame and struggle with her alcohol and how hiding her addiction was causing difficulty in her new relationship.

Sally was ready to change, but she couldn't stop the cycle of drinking to manage her feelings. Keeping it a secret only increased the tension—and the drinking. She risked opening up with me and sharing her fears and struggles, and tears of relief overflowed as she let herself be heard and seen with openness and love.

Together, Sally and I explored how alcohol was nourishing her. Whenever we have an addiction, whether it is to a drug, overeating, or to judgmental thinking, it helps to disrupt the routine by naming the gifts of our old behaviors out loud and thanking the addiction for the ways it has nourished us. Then we can look at new ways of nourishing ourselves.

Next, Sally and I talked about how else she could get nourishment when she felt alone or scared. She realized that hiding her problem from her friends and from her new relationship was only exacerbating the problem, and it was time for her to start a long-term nourishing project by taking new actions. She started by sharing her addiction with those closest to her and creating a circle of people whom she could trust to help her learn to nourish herself in a new way.

Sally committed to doing one nourishing thing for herself before bed (reading poetry, taking a bath, breathing into her belly) and to calling someone from her list of allies if she started craving alcohol, so that they could support her in opening and being present with her fears, rather than abandoning herself to alcohol. Over time, Sally learned to hold herself in a nourishing way, and her need for alcohol as a source of nourishment dissolved.

Here is my story about a behavior that once felt nourishing and how I learned to resist short-term nourishment and gain long-term health.

I remember a time when my body loved sugar. I was working the night shift at a newspaper, and I consumed a great deal of sugar and caffeine to keep me going. I was young and wired and could go for days with little sleep. I was physically healthy, rarely sick, and excited about my life.

One day I experienced a drastic shift. After ten years of drinking Coca-Cola with impunity, I started to feel lethargic and sick. I soon noticed a relationship between my level of sugar consumption and not feeling well. When I really paid attention to my body, I realized I had to stop eating sugar. I fought this realization for a while. How could this be possible? I'd always eaten sugar. But for two years, if I ate a bite of pie or took a sip of any sugary drink, my body let me know it was unhappy with my choices. Something that had once felt very nourishing to me was now toxic. For a long time, I still craved sugar; it felt like such great short-term nourishment! Yet as I focused on long-term nourishment, my body healed, and it stopped yearning for sugar.

Similarly, you can track and learn what is nourishing to you and what is not. You may find patterns and behaviors that were once nourishing but now weaken you. Something that others say is nourishing may not be what you need in the moment. Keep your long-term vision focused on your greater intent as you make new choices in the moment.

Sometimes nurturing yourself is doing exactly the opposite of what your habitual reaction would be. Such acts will not feel completely comfortable in the moment, but they are long-term nourishment. If you are a perfectionist, a nourishing act might be to allow yourself to make mistakes and celebrate them. If you are afraid to make choices, a nourishing act might be to make a definite decision and follow through on it each day. If you are anxious, a nourishing act might be to focus on your breath every five minutes. If you are used to doing everything by yourself, asking a friend to simply hold you might be nourishing. If you always rely on others to make you feel better, spending time alone might be nourishing.

Sometimes a simple act of nourishment will reveal deep hungers and pain. As you begin to nourish yourself, you may discover that a huge part of your structure is, for example, based on believing that you do not deserve love. When you start feeding a part of yourself that has been starved and cut off, the hunger can seem more intense. Reassure yourself that you will not abandon yourself again and that you will nurture and support yourself.

Feeding the Frozen Aspects of Yourself

I spent years trying to ignore and think my way out of the fear, sense of scarcity, and grief in my body. All my nourishing energy went toward figuring out how I could make my difficult feelings go away. I nurtured ways to avoid pain and ignore the terror that would creep in. I believed, "If only I could run faster than this, it will go away. I would be okay if only the fear would leave me alone."

Slowly, I learned to stop running away; I learned to become still and go into my body rather than ignoring it. This was difficult.

I recognized my level of self-abandonment when I did yoga by myself for the first time. As I held the first pose, I wept for no apparent reason. My body was terrified and confused but also relieved that I was bringing my attention to it.

Where have you abandoned or ignored your body?

One of the main reasons we have lost the art of nourishing ourselves is our desire to hide from old pain. Each of us has a child trapped within our structure, frozen in time. Most of our emotional reactions in the present are the reactions of this child, not the adult. Cleaning and opening reveal these old patterns and reactions and the immense emotional energy they carry. Nourishing heals these places.

Your structure is held in place by the energy of old, stuck agreements and stories from your past. When you open to all of your being, you embrace the angry toddler, the frightened child, and the gawky teenager. Instead of ignoring the frightened child or wishing the gawky teenager would go away, you can nourish each aspect of yourself. Just as you learn to nourish yourself in the moment at each part of the cycle, you also learn to nourish all of your various ages.

Can you make space for the angry toddler to discover what lies beneath the anger? What does the frightened child need from you? How can you reassure the gawky teenager?

Befriending the body is one of your greatest sources of power. To truly befriend and nourish the body, you need two skills: listening with unconditional love and creating appropriate boundaries.

Listening with Unconditional Love

Our bodies store all of our old agreements. The crucial thing to remember is that the agreements you discover in your body—the fears, the paralysis, the insecurities—are coming from a child. The only way to shift this part of the structure is to listen to and nourish your child. You do not need to know exactly what the agreement was, but you do need to honor and create a safe space for the child.

The adult part of you may think, "That is ridiculous. I can't believe that agreement!" Remember that the child made the agreement with a child's mind. Sometimes these agreements are made even before you can speak. They are body memories and fears, not mere mental constructs.

When you listen, when you open wide, you become larger than the child and can step into the role of nurturing parent. When you ask your child, "What do you need?" you begin the journey of nourishing the child into growing up.

Often the act of nourishing is as simple as choosing to stay home one evening, but often our resistance to honoring the child is huge. When we do not listen, the child either goes numb and silent or increases the intensity of the feeling, until we forget our adult self and become the child again.

When you cut off the child, you also cut off your creativity and joy. No matter how hard you try to keep the child silent, eventually your child will emerge strongly. Something triggers an old memory, and suddenly you are taken over by huge emotions, body memories, and fears. You then begin reacting to the world around you from the hurt child's point of view. As you have probably seen, living from the hurt child's perspective creates chaos as the child tries to keep itself safe and get its needs met in an adult world.

If something feels uncomfortable, nourish yourself through it. Gently nudge yourself forward, rather than forcing yourself. Saying, "Let's sit in this uncomfortable place just a little bit longer" will allow you to keep your awareness as you delve into the difficult places within.

Nourishing is about honoring all parts of self. You can be a successful, respected businessperson and a grief-stricken three-year-old. You can be on a spiritual journey and be having two-year-old tantrums inside. One does not negate the other. Your deepest foundation holds all of you.

All your parts create who you are. You are a multi-dimensional being with complementary as well as contradictory emotions and beliefs occurring on different levels at the same time. The rebellious ten-year-old in you may inspire you to create art that no one has seen before, yet also cause you to be irresponsible and difficult in relationships. The six-year-old you, who was the apple of your father's eye until you got buckteeth and he began to make fun of you, now desperately wants a man to love you as you are. Yet no other person, or anything else outside you for that matter, can take away the pain. Although the adult in you knows the reality of relationships and can discern when a man is being loving, to the six-year-old, every man is a disappointment.

I have learned to listen and slow things down when the child starts speaking. This does not mean that everything in my life comes to a halt, but that I open wider. I stretch. I expand, so I can be parent and child, so I can love and be loved, while continuing my life.

My clue that my child needs attention is a strong bodily sensation or a loud, fearful mind. I usually go for a walk and ask myself, "What do you need?" The child has learned that she can trust me, so she talks to me pretty quickly now. "I need to be held." And I will imagine holding her, sending her love. Sometimes she says, "I want you to stop taking that risk; it scares me." And with love I will tell her, "This is very important to me. I know it is scary, but I am right here with you."

The biggest place of pain you create is when you abandon yourself. Nourishing is about showing up for yourself, no matter what. Others may abandon you, betray you, dislike you. This is a painful truth about life. But the greatest pain comes when you abandon, betray, or dislike *yourself*. The greatest healing comes when you reclaim, nourish, and honor yourself, exactly as you are. Part of this healing comes from learning to make appropriate boundaries for yourself and your child.

Boundaries as Nourishment

Creating a new structure entails building a safe container where you can heal old pain. Opening does not mean letting go of all boundaries. In fact, boundaries are a vital part of nourishing. One of the biggest gifts of the element of earth is clear boundaries. Most boundaries are limitations based on fear and are used to defend a position. But boundaries made out of love and concern for your own growth and wholeness help keep you open.

Creating nourishing boundaries gives you a container in which to open and explore what lies within yourself. You can make boundaries out of fear, to keep out experiences and emotions that you do not like, but this action does not nourish you; rather, it causes you to close down and keep everything out, both frightening and good. When you make boundaries out of self-respect and honor where you are in the moment, you can stay open and allow nourishment to enter.

A very simple practice for setting a boundary is to take

time for yourself. If you are serious about your return to center, you should be alone with yourself on a regular basis. Being in nature once a week, sitting quietly in the mornings, or taking yourself out to walk under the stars once a month are all ways of being with yourself. Carve out and nourish your time to look within, to become more intimate with yourself.

Do not use this time to judge or criticize yourself, no matter how bad you are feeling. Be with your child or your gawky teenager. Ask them what they want, and nourish their deepest needs, beneath the fear and reaction. Notice the urge to hold your old, cracking foundation together. Practice sitting with any feelings and discomfort in your body while you nourish yourself with your breath and your presence.

Making a safe container for the child does not mean giving your child everything he or she wants. Children need boundaries that arise out of love. Imagine if your child said, "I am going to eat the whole chocolate cake!" How would you make an appropriate boundary? Sometimes your child wants to do things that are not nourishing. Learn to set clear, loving boundaries.

You can learn to set internal, loving boundaries with the hurt child so that you do not continue the external cycle of drama and blaming others. It rarely helps to throw your pain unconsciously onto someone else, even though it might feel great in the moment. It is a short-term fix, but it may be necessary when you first get in touch with the child. Move toward expressing the emotion in a safe way first, then sharing it later.

You might say to your child, "Yes, honey, I know that you want to scream and hurt those people who seem to be hurting you. Let's go for a long walk first and throw rocks at the water, then talk to those people later." Or "Yes, it looks like those people really meant to hurt you. But they are just in pain themselves; it is not about us. Let's go take a bath and cry out some of this old pain and fear."

Creating a container means noticing your surroundings and choosing a safe place to express what is inside. You cannot always express what is inside you at any given moment. You may have an incident at work where you get emotionally triggered by something and feel a welling up of old pain. If you want the child to trust you, follow through and create a safe space at a later time. Trust builds from authentic listening and appropriate action. You can say to yourself, "I know this hurts, and we will make a safe space to cry later."

Trust also grows when you set appropriate external boundaries. It is an art to learn to say no with an open heart and a soft belly. It may take a while to build up to creating a firm yet openhearted boundary.

Imagine that you need to set a boundary with someone: a coworker who constantly interrupts you at your job. For days you have sent her subtle clues that you do not want to be interrupted. You have ignored her, invited her to talk with you after work, gossiped to others in your office about how this person is driving you crazy. The only thing left is to tell her not to interrupt you.

There are many different ways you can set this

boundary. You can postpone setting the boundary for a long time, then blow up at her. You can get angry with her and shut your door whenever you see her coming. You can get someone else to tell her to stop interrupting you. You can tell her the boss is getting upset at you for not finishing your work on time.

Notice how setting boundaries feels in your body. How does it feel when you do not tell others what you need but instead hope they figure it out? How does it feel when you judge and become angry with them and simply shut them out of your life? How does it feel when you blame someone else because you need things to be different?

These methods might work, but they cause you to close down. They do not nourish you. They do not teach you to speak your truth.

Learning to set boundaries without rejecting or projecting onto others, or needing them to be any different from who they are, takes time. One approach is to practice in small doses. Imagine setting a boundary with the interrupting coworker while keeping yourself open and present. How would this look and feel?

You might say something like, "I notice that you tend to interrupt me a lot while I'm speaking. I'm guessing that you are really excited to share what you have to say, but it makes me feel frustrated and not heard. Would you please wait until I've finished speaking to share your point of view?" Practice by saying this out loud to your imaginary coworker. Stay connected to her by looking into her eyes, and breath through any discomfort or fear.

Now pick a situation in your own life where a boundary would be helpful. Write out what you want to say and practice saying it out loud, exploring how to keep yourself connected to the person through eye contact and connected to yourself through your breath and presence.

You may be afraid to set boundaries for fear of hurting or upsetting others. This is short-term thinking. Not setting a simple boundary may feel easier in the moment, but the long-term ramifications are vast. One result is that you stop trusting yourself. The message you are giving your body is: "Your needs are not important."

Create boundaries to nourish yourself, rather than to make others behave a certain way. Boundaries are not for controlling others. "I want you to stop that behavior; it hurts me!" is not a boundary but a demand. "I feel hurt when you get angry" implies that their anger is hurting you. The truth is their anger is their anger, and your hurt is your hurt. Let them be angry, be open to your own hurt, and consciously choose your reaction. This is easier said than done, for in the heat of the moment you may react rather than choose. Again, move toward staying open and nourishing yourself, no matter what others are doing.

Making clear boundaries is about taking responsibility for yourself and your needs. Boundaries help you prevent taking on the problems of others.

You may not like what your current boundaries are. Your child may say, "I really need not to be sexual for a while." Your adult may not like that idea. You can try negotiating and asking the child what it really needs. You may find that you need to honor what the child is asking for and that you are willing to set that boundary, even though you are afraid about what your partner will say. At other times, you may learn that you are not as open as you want to be and that you still have rigid, fear-based boundaries about certain issues. Notice that you are a work in progress, and honor the current moment. Stretch yourself, but honor your limitations and boundaries.

It can be frightening to set boundaries. When you first start setting them, pay attention to what arises. Guilt, fear of rejection, shame, or insecurity may all arise to haunt you. Do not nourish these emotions; instead, nourish the strength of your being that is beneath them. Know they are passing; they are from an old time.

Your goal is to move away from nourishing your old structure and toward nurturing your authentic center. Do not be surprised if a simple act of nourishing yourself or setting a boundary brings up big emotions. Remember, you are taking energy away from your old foundation and placing it into a new foundation. The old structure may fight and scream and try in myriad ways to hook your attention. Keep going back to your intent and your four new foundational anchors connected with the four elements. Remind yourself that you are creating a new foundation to build a conscious house for yourself with much more room for your spirit.

Use the energy of your old foundation to nourish your new one. As you remove your attachment to the old structures, you free up energy. You can then take this energy and compost it into the soil of your being. There is no fight here, only the intent to allow the rigid and painful parts of your structure to dissolve into fertile compost for new growth.

Practices

 Grounding

It is very nourishing to connect your physical body to the earth through a process called grounding. Grounding settles and energizes you. It helps you release nervous or stuck energy and allows you to feel the strength and ease that comes from being supported unconditionally.

To ground yourself, sit comfortably with your feet flat on the floor, or sit cross-legged on the ground. Breathe your awareness down into the base of your spine. Let your belly be soft. Imagine yourself as a tree, with roots that go deep into the earth and branches that stretch up to the sky. Let your spine form roots that spread out into the soil. Your branches reach up from the crown of your head and into the sky. Feel how your physical body, the trunk of your tree, rests perfectly between your roots and branches.

Imagine that you can breathe energy and vitality through your roots up into your body. Breathe this energy all the way through your body, and send it out through your branches to the sky. Now imagine breathing the openness and vastness of space into your branches.

Breathe this energy through your body and down into the earth.

With each breath, allow yourself to be held and supported by earth and sky. Feel the unlimited amount of energy available to you. Allow this energy to saturate every cell of your body and create a sense of wholeness and connection. Let your mind be quiet, and let your body relax.

When you are finished, take three deep breaths into your heart and gently release your image of roots and branches.

As part of your grounding practice, also set aside a little time each day to listen to your body. Go for a slow walk in nature, do yoga, or simply sit quietly and tune in to yourself. Tell your body that you are willing to listen and hear what it has to tell you. Invite your body to speak and share its fears and its wisdom.

Often your body will keep amplifying its messages until you hear it, or it will stop talking to you altogether. When you first begin to slow down and listen to your body, it may refuse to speak or only yell at you for not paying attention. Be patient with yourself. Your body holds tremendous knowledge. Let it know that you are willing to spend time nourishing its deepest needs. When you get a message, image, or feeling from your body, honor it while delving into the core of your truth. It may take time to reestablish a relationship with your body. Be patient and stay present with yourself.

Tools for Nourishing

Write down ten acts that nourish you; ten separate things that make you happy and feel good about yourself. Here are some examples:

playing with my dog

hugging someone

doing yoga

taking a long walk

reading spiritual books

being in silence

performing a ritual

taking a hot bath

watching children play

dancing

Write down your ten nourishing acts on separate index cards. You can also draw them or make ten mini-collages with photographs and magazine pictures.

Start by picking one of your cards each day and doing the action it suggests. Pay attention to how it nourishes you and what you feel. This will give you a template to draw on later.

When you have completed all ten cards, begin to use these cards to explore opening yourself to more nourishment. Think of something that causes you to close down—a memory of your ex-husband or ex-wife, a fear of something in the future, or a situation at home. Pick one of the cards and focus on it. Weave the two feelings together; for example, take a hot bath while thinking about your ex. Relax into the practices and feelings that open you, and create a little bit more opening in your body for the situations and feelings that cause you to close down. What if you stayed open to a stressful situation and nourished yourself? What would the outcome be?

Start with small occurrences, and build your way up to larger events.

When you are in crisis and want to nourish yourself, pick one of your cards. Put the card into action, either by doing it or meditating on what it feels like when you do it. Let it seep into your body. When you have the most resistance to using the card is the best time to take action! Keep inviting yourself to open and be nourished, even if the opening is only a tiny crack at first.

Connecting to the Element of Earth

The act of nourishing a plant is a great way to connect to the element of earth in your everyday life. To learn about the cycle of growth, nurture a plant from a seedling until it is fully grown.

Planting seeds is best done in the spring or early summer, though it will work any time of the year with enough light and warmth. If you travel a lot, you can use a plant that doesn't need much water as your connection to earth.

Get a cup or planter box, and buy some seeds (tomatoes or sunflowers work well). You could also buy a little herb garden starter kit, available in many garden stores.

When you plant the seeds, set an intent for what you want to nourish in your own life. For example:

"With this seed, I set my intent to nourish my desire to have more friendship in my life."

"Just as I commit to taking care of this plant, I commit to taking care of my own need for good food and water."

"May I nourish the soul of my being just as I nourish this seedling."

Now plant your seeds or repot a plant: Get your hands in the soil! You may want to write your intent and place it on or nearby the container. Each time you water the plant, touch the soil and ask for a blessing on your *own* soil. Giving your new plant the consistent care it needs will remind you that your physical self needs the same attention and love. You will learn a lot about yourself and the process of growth as you nourish your plant.

As your plant gets bigger, you may need to repot it or find a good place to plant it outside. Always feel free to start over if something happens to your plant. Make it a practice until you have come to know intimately the nourishing power of earth.

Inner Guidance

Earth Visualization for Creating a New Container

Your fourth guardian is the element of earth. From earth you learn the art of nurturing—the right use of your physical body.

Get your body comfortable, either sitting or standing, and take some deep breaths into your belly. Imagine yourself standing in the middle of your stone circle. Greet your symbols for the elements of air, fire, and water. Turn to face the final quarter in your circle, and ask for guidance and energy from the element of earth to give you the grace and intent to nurture your deepest self.

Invite an earth guide to join you and support you in living from your core foundation. Be open to how that guide may appear. Your earth guide may be an animal, a person you know, or a stranger. It may be a quiet voice in your head or a knowing in your body. Your guardian of earth may not come to you immediately, but later in a dream or while you are in the middle of your day, earth may show its many forms to you. Pray for the power to nourish your being and create sacred boundaries.

When you feel complete, ask for a symbol to represent this new anchor, and place it in the final direction of your circle.

For your altar, pick an object to represent earth, and place it in the final direction on the outside of the circle.

You can represent earth with a rock, a statue of a person, or any object that pleases you. Set your intent to use all of the elements and their gifts to guide you to become deeply intimate with yourself, and manifest an inner container that reflects the strength of your center.

7

The Fifth Element:
Beyond Structure

Be humble for you are made of earth. Be noble for you are made of stars.

—Serbian proverb

When you consciously work with the elements of air, fire, water, and earth, you create a circle of support around your old belief system. Each gift of the elements is a tool to reclaim your own stuck energy and release what does not serve you. Now, for the second time, you'll build a structure, but this new structure is a temple constructed with awareness and joy.

You have everything you need within you to reclaim a sacred, possibility-filled life. The ancient teachings of the elements are always available, offering solace and direction during even the toughest times. It may take time, great patience, and much compassion, but it *is* possible. The transformation will lead you from living in a messy, cramped room to living in a huge, light-filled temple.

At any moment, you can open your eyes to the truth. A magnificent, invisible temple surrounds the small room within yourself that you hide in. Looking from the inside out, you see yourself trapped in one tiny, gray room with a locked door. From the outside looking in, you see yourself curled in the corner of one room in a vast, many-roomed chamber of colors, textures, and space. And the door is open.

All the walls within your temple are alive. They breathe. They whisper to you, "You are huge. You are eternal. You are magnificent. You have gifts to share. Come out of your self-created room and claim your temple."

Your ears are tuned to the walls of your tiny room, which whisper, "This is all there is. Stay here, stay safe. You do not deserve to be bigger. You are already too big. Do not challenge the strength of these walls."

Nevertheless, you manage for seconds or days at a time to slip out and see the vastness around you. At these times, the little room of your life dissolves, and you are awed by the vision of eternity around you. Or you consciously step through the door and discover a new dream beyond what you thought possible.

The transition between living in your familiar prison and living as big as the sky depends on a conscious use of the four elements. The elements and their gifts act as a foundation to pull your energy out of the unconscious rooms in your life. From this place, you can use these four anchors to weave a sacred base for a fifth point above your circle—pure essence. This magical place is the synergy of all four elements working together to create the fifth element, a direct connection to the infinite creative source of life.

When you live from the fifth element, you step into what you were always meant to become: a conscious temple, a direct reflection of spirit.

The first stage to stepping beyond your cramped rooms is to become conscious of your confinement. The second stage is building a new frame to surround your old structure. The third stage is pulling your energy from the old structure into your new, larger structure. And the fourth stage is realizing that there is not and never was any structure at all. This structureless place is the realm of the fifth element, or what the Toltec call the *nagual.*

The structures we are talking about are created by your mind and energy. They are real and tangible and strong, and they are also illusions. Since they are created by the mind, they can be dissolved by the mind at a moment's notice. They are as real as you make them.

Once this new structure is in place, you will see your old structure with new eyes. The same emotions, fears, and disaster mind will be present, but instead of living them, you will witness them with love and perhaps even a smile on your face. Instead of using your mind, energy, emotions, and body against yourself, you will see all manifestations of fear and doubt as precious resources, as nuggets of potential energy that are simply trapped and waiting to be freed.

You are a vast, always-centered, magical being. But your attention is hooked by the fears of the mind. The way out is to realize once and for all that you are pure, unhindered energy. You are a wild child of the universe, let loose in a magnificent playground to create whatever you dream possible. If you do not remember this with every fiber of your being by the time you read the end of this paragraph, I suggest you start by building a larger container for yourself, step by step, using the Four Elements of Change.

All humans have the ability to dance into the unknown and move beyond all structures in an instant. This could happen today, and it could happen the moment you die. This is the mystery. In the meantime, why not remodel your cramped quarters?

As you move into a larger conscious structure, your heart and soul expand to hold more love and energy. You move from limitations to possibilities.

This is not a one-way journey but a path that will

move back and forth between your old and new structures and infinity. There will be days or weeks or months at a time when you will forget the new structure and move back into your cramped room. It will seem as if nothing has changed, as if all the work you have done was in vain, as if you are a failure. But the new structure is there, waiting for you, supporting you.

There will be days or weeks or months at a time when you will live from your new structure, forgetting that you ever lived any other way. You will feel balanced and present, open and nourished. Your life will unfold magically. Then one day you will find yourself unexpectedly slammed back into the middle of your old structure, or you will discover yourself slowly sliding, without a foothold to stop you, back into an old pattern. Can you keep your eyes open? If you can, you will learn, and you will be able to bring energy and more awareness back into your new structure. If you plummet into complete forgetfulness, forgive yourself when you wake up again, and review what you have learned.

What I have seen is that as I have invested more and more of my energy in my new structure, the transitions between old and new are quicker. This felt a little strange at first. I would feel centered and balanced, get triggered by someone being upset with me at work or a fear of being abandoned, go into fear and judgment, but then quickly pop out of it again. Part of me would wonder why I was no longer upset.

I sometimes find myself staring at the place where an old structure used to be, wondering where it went, feeling awkward without it. There can be phantom limbs in our structure, places that are cleared out but that still hold a resonance, a memory. Eventually this, too, will dissolve. Do your best not to feed the old structure again; instead, allow yourself to be uncomfortable with the newness.

The move into the new structure completes the journey for some; for others it is only a beginning. You may choose to remodel your room, paint the walls and add some nice furnishings, and feel complete. Or you may look toward creating an entirely new structure and moving into a bigger space. Perhaps you will even look beyond this structure, choose to release all structures, and merge with the fifth element of infinity. Whether your focus is on a minor remodel or on a dissolution of all structures, the steps are the same. Perceive. Clean. Open. Nourish. Step by step, one moment at a time. From the new structure, you will be better able to live from your center.

Do your best to not get overwhelmed by the task ahead of you. Keep your focus in the moment, on the current action. When you first begin to work with the gifts of the elements, start small. Pick one element at a time to practice. You can pick the element you feel most comfortable with or the one you feel most uncomfortable with. Remember, the elements are not linear; rather, they form a circle. The entry point to your healing lies anywhere within this circle.

For example, if you choose fire, the element of cleaning, give yourself small tasks to accomplish during the day. Set your intent and ask for guidance to help you learn about cleaning. Create touchstones to remind you of your focus: "Every time I light a candle or turn on a light, I will check in to see if there is anything within me that I need to clean out." "This week I will light a candle, then clean some part of my house that I've been putting off cleaning to represent cleaning a part of myself I've been avoiding." "I am going to do one of the fire practices this week, a little each day."

As your energy shifts from one structure to another, a new world will open up. You will have the energy to create what you want. But do not try to skip any of the steps. It is better to be clear and systematic in building a new structure. Create a strong foundation with each of the elements. Really learn the art of perception. Practice the art of cleaning. Explore the art of opening. Manifest the art of nourishing in all aspects of your life.

In this way, you are in service to your true self, to your center. Your center lies within the very middle of your old structure, hidden deep in the foundation, buried under layers and layers of old beliefs and habits. It is pure and untouched, a jewel waiting to be brought into the light. Creating a new structure gives you the space to see the jewel within you and the energy to unearth it.

As you reconfigure your old structure, the jewel within you shines more brightly. You begin to see the unique, precious being that you are. Comparison drops away as you value the perfection of who you are, right in this moment. You are the complex, multifaceted jewel, held by a structure of love. The structure of fear gets sandwiched between. You see without a doubt that it does not have a chance of survival. Getting triggered or going into self-doubt and fear is no longer a disaster but an exciting opportunity to reclaim more energy, to shine more brightly.

The goal is not outside yourself but within. What element can you use today to create more space for the brightness of your center? In this moment, how can you move into a larger structure and give yourself room to grow?

Gradually, your perceptions will begin to shift again. You will get flashes of another reality, an even larger vision. The center jewel of you, the unique, awesome, powerful light of you, is only a tiny star in a much bigger galaxy. Your nature is not to live in a limited structure but to know yourself as part of the web of all possibilities. You become both a star in the temple of spirit and the temple itself. You become the fifth element, pure nonduality and presence.

Right now, you are an infinite temple of life. You are a vast being. You are also a frightened child hiding in a corner, yearning for approval. Hold all of yourself, free and fearful, in the palms of your hands. In this way, you become a Spirit Weaver, weaving all of you—the sacred and mundane—into the fullness of your potential, clear and centered.

Recommended
Further Reading

Abelar, Taisha. *The Sorcerers' Crossing*. New York: Viking Arcana, 1992.

Beck, Renee, and Sydney Barbara Metrick. *The Art of Ritual: Creating and Performing Ceremonies for Growth and Change*. Berkeley, CA: Celestial Arts, 2003.

Blanton, Brad. *Radical Honesty: How to Transform Your Life*. New York: Dell Publications, 1996.

Castaneda, Carlos. *Journey to Ixtlan: The Lessons of Don Juan*. New York: Simon and Schuster, 1972.

———. *The Power of Silence: Further Lessons of Don Juan*. New York: Simon and Schuster, 1987.

———. *The Wheel of Time: Shamans of Mexico and Their Thoughts about Life, Death, and the Universe*. New York: Washington Square Press, 2001.

Dibble, David. *The New Agreements in the Workplace: Releasing the Human Spirit*. New York: Emeritus, 2002.

Kingston, Karen. *Clear Your Clutter with Feng Shui.* New York: Broadway Books, 1999.

Mares, Théun. *This Darned Elusive Happiness.* Cape Town, Great Britain: Lionheart, 1999.

Prechtel, Martín. *Secrets of the Talking Jaguar: Memoirs from the Living Heart of a Mayan Village.* New York: Jeremy P. Tarcher, 1999.

Nelson, Mary Carroll. *Beyond Fear: A Toltec Guide to Freedom and Joy.* Tulsa, OK: Council Oak Books, 1997.

Noble, Vicki. *Shakti Woman: Feeling Our Fire, Healing Our World.* San Francisco: HarperSanFrancisco, 1991.

Rosenberg, Marshall B. *Nonviolent Communication: A Language of Compassion.* Del Mar, CA: PuddleDancer Press, 1999.

Ruiz, Miguel. *The Four Agreements: A Practical Guide to Personal Freedom.* San Rafael, CA: Amber-Allen Publishing, 1997.

———. *The Mastery of Love: A Practical Guide to the Art of Relationship.* San Rafael, CA: Amber-Allen Publishing, 1999.

Sanchez, Victor. *Teachings of Don Carlos: Practical Applications of the Works of Carlos Castaneda.* Translated by Robert Nelson. Santa Fe, NM: Bear & Co., 1995.

Starhawk. *The Spiral Dance: A Rebirth of the Ancient Religion of the Great Goddess.* San Francisco: HarperSanFransisco, 1999.

Stone, Hal, and Sidra Winkelman. *Embracing Our Selves: The Voice Dialogue Manual.* San Rafael, CA: New World Library, 1989.

Tunneshende, Merilyn. *Don Juan and the Art of Sexual Energy: The Rainbow Serpent of the Toltecs.* Rochester, VT: Bear & Co., 2001.

Vigil, Bernadette. *Mastery of Awareness: Living the Agreements.* Rochester, VT: Bear & Co., 2001.

Weinstein, Marion. *Positive Magic: Ancient Metaphysical Techniques for Modern Lives.* Franklin Lakes, NJ: New Page, 2002.

HeatherAsh Amara is the founder of Toci—the Toltec Center of Creative Intent based in Austin, Texas— which fosters local and global communities that support authenticity, awareness, and awakening. HeatherAsh is dedicated to inspiring depth, creativity, and joy by sharing the most potent tools from a variety of world traditions. She studied and taught extensively with don Miguel Ruiz, author of *The Four Agreements,* and continues to teach with the Ruiz family.

HeatherAsh was raised in Southeast Asia and has traveled the world since childhood; she is continually inspired by the diversity and beauty of human expression and experience. She brings this openhearted, inclusive worldview to her writings and teachings, which are a rich blend of Toltec wisdom, European shamanism, Buddhism, and Native American ceremony.

Made in the USA
Middletown, DE
01 September 2016